South Carolina *and* Barbados Connections

Selections from the *South Carolina Historical Magazine*

Second Edition

Introduction by
Stephen G. Hoffius

Home House Press
Charleston, S.C.
2021

South Carolina *and* Barbados Connections
Selections from the South Carolina Historical Magazine

Second Edition

ISBN: 978-1-952248-83-2 (trade paper)

Published by:
HOME HOUSE PRESS

109 Broad Street
Charleston, S.C. 29401
www.HomeHousePress.com

For information on
The South Carolina Historical Magazine or
The South Carolina Historical Society:

South Carolina Historical Society
100 Meeting Street
Charleston, S.C. 29401
(843) 723-3225
www. SouthCarolinaHistoricalSociety.org

Printed in the U.S.A.

Contents

Introduction
by Stephen G. Hoffius v

The Barbadians In Early South Carolina
by Jno. P. Thomas, Jr. 1

The English Sugar Islands and the Founding of South Carolina
by Richard S. Dunn 19

Colonial South Carolina and the Caribbean Connection
by Jack P. Greene 33

Review of *The Barbados-Carolina Connection*
by George C. Rogers, Jr. & George W. Williams 53

The South Carolina Slave Laws Reconsidered, 1670-1700
by Thomas J. Little 59

Barbadian Settlers in Early Carolina: Historiographical Notes
by Kinloch Bull 75

Errata 86
About the Authors 87
Index 89

Introduction

For more than a century, the South Carolina Historical Society has highlighted the close ties between South Carolina and Barbados. In 1897 the Society published a 476-page volume entitled *The Shaftesbury Papers and Other Records Relating to Carolina and the First Settlement on Ashley River Prior to the Year 1676.* Most of these records were drawn from documents deposited by the earl of Shaftesbury, primary architect of the South Carolina settlement, in the British Public Record Office. (The volume was reprinted by Home House Press in 2010.) Much of the story of the efforts of Barbadians (today called Bajans) to settle South Carolina in the late seventeenth century is told in *The Shaftesbury Papers,* still the most important published source on the matter. So great was the Barbados influence that Peter Wood in *Black Majority* called South Carolina "The Colony of a Colony."

As with any historical subject, researchers have relied on the work of their predecessors (which sometimes causes problems, as Kinloch Bull explains in this volume). Wood, for instance, frequently cites *The Shaftesbury Papers,* as does John P. Thomas Jr. in his 1930 article "The Barbadians in Early South Carolina" in the Historical Society's journal *South Carolina Historical and Genealogical Magazine.* (In 1952 the title of the publication was changed to the *South Carolina Historical Magazine.)* That was the first major article in the *Magazine* to examine the Carolina-Barbados connection.

As one can see by the six items reprinted here, researchers in the last century have attempted to expand our understanding of that connection and to gather more details. Yes, the researchers acknowledge, many of the original South Carolina settlers, white and black, came from Barbados, but did they live there or merely stop in Barbados on their trips across the Atlantic? Yes, the South Carolina slave codes were based on Bajan antecedents, but which specific elements? How did Bajan economic interests compare with those of other Caribbean islands? What parts of the South Carolina culture drew from Bajan roots—the architecture? Language?

Important research on all of these subjects and more is being conducted today in archives in both South Carolina and Barbados. Institutions in both places are encouraging individuals to travel from America to the island nation and vice versa both for pleasure and for expanding our historical knowledge. The Barbados Tourism Authority led the way in this effort in 1985 by organizing a team of people in the Caribbean tourism industry to visit Charleston to research the shared history. That visit paved the way for others to start looking more seriously into the connecting history. The Carolina-Caribbean Association in Charleston (now defunct) helped to bring people together in the 1990s, as did the Barbados-Carolina Committee of the Barbados Ministry of

Tourism Authority; the South Carolina National Heritage Corridor; and the College of Charleston's program on the Carolina Lowcountry and the Atlantic World. Now the University of the West Indies and the Barbados Museum and Historical Society have become involved to share information and support. Private groups and organizations such as the Charleston Museum has arranged group visits to the island to learn more about the connections.

In November 1998 a group of South Carolinians, drawn together by Mrs. Rhoda Green, a Barbados native who lives in Charleston and served as president of the Carolina-Caribbean Association for over fifteen years, traveled to Barbados for tours, lectures, meetings, and a generous outpouring of Bajan hospitality. (Mrs. Green is now Barbados's honorary consul to South Carolina.) During that visit, references repeatedly were made to various writings on the Carolina-Barbados connection. Typically, no one had those writings at their fingertips. In an effort to encourage additional research on these important ties, the South Carolina Historical Society prepared a photocopied collection of items which had appeared in the pages of the *South Carolina Historical Magazine.* Those contents make up this volume, published by Home House Press of Charleston, which previously published a book of articles from the *Historical Magazine* on the American Civil War. (Much of this introduction appeared first in that 1998 volume.) There are many additional references in the *Historical Magazine* and important articles in other periodicals and books. But these, written by eminent scholars, should be enough to provide background on the Carolina-Barbados connection, to encourage further readings, and to stimulate additional research (not to mention vacation trips).

The shared histories of Barbados and Carolina are more visible today than ever before. In the town of Speightstown, Barbados, the Arlington House has been fully restored and now operates as a museum; some researchers have suggested that the house represents an architectural style that inspired Charleston's single-house design. The Bush Hill House outside Bridgetown, where nineteen-year-old George Washington stayed in 1751 during his only trip outside the United States, has been restored and named the George Washington House; in Barbados Washington contracted smallpox, protecting him when the disease was ravaging American troops during the Revolution. In 2006 the Warren family purchased St. Nicholas Abbey, the 350-year-old Jacobean home, sugar-cane plantation, and rum factory on Barbados's east coast, and has restored much of the site; one of the previous owners, Sir John Yeamans, moved to Carolina and served as one of the first governors. On rare occasions, the marching band of the Barbados Police Band still plays "Carolina Laurel" in honor of the Black Carolina Corps, a unit of black troops raised by the British army shortly before the troops evacuated Charleston in December 1782; after the Revolution the Black Carolina Corps continued to serve in various British Caribbean possessions. And at Charles Towne Landing, the original location of Charleston, a wonderful new historical display details the story of the settlers who came to Carolina from Barbados in the 1670s.

On June 25, 2011, the World Heritage Committee placed Barbados's "Bridgetown and its Garrison" on UNESCO's World Heritage List; the site is described as "an outstanding example of British colonial architecture which testifies to the spread of Great Britain's Atlantic colonial empire," which, of course, before the American Revolution, included the Carolinas.

No one can fully appreciate South Carolina history without an understanding of the Barbados history that led to the colony's settlement. In the same way, much of the history of Barbados can be found in the outreach of her residents—to North America, South America, and the islands of the Caribbean. Our histories and our cultures, as the following items make clear, are closely intertwined. Even after more than a hundred years of research about that relationship, much of it we are only now uncovering.

STEPHEN G. HOFFIUS
Charleston, South Carolina

The Barbadians In Early South Carolina

BY JNO. P. THOMAS, JR.

Originally published in the
South Carolina Historical and Archaeological Magazine
Volume 31, Number 2 (April 1930)

The history of the early settlement of South Carolina is intimately connected with the island of Barbados.[1] It is an interesting episode in the light of all the surrounding circumstances and in view of all the influences that came into play. These influences had their effect upon the social, political and religious development of South Carolina.

This island was probably first discovered by the Portuguese in their voyages from Brazil, but it was visited by the British as early as 1605. The first settlement by them was in 1624. Since its first occupation by the British, the island has known no flag but the British flag and it has never once wavered in its staunch allegiance to the British crown. It is said to be the oldest of the British possessions. It is the most easterly of the West India Islands. It is well within the tropics, being in latitude 13°4' north. It has an area of one hundred sixty-six square miles and is twenty-one miles in length and fourteen and a half in its broadest part. It is a coral island and its highest elevations are only moderately sized hills. There are few streams on the island. The climate is healthful, the temperature stable. For eight months in the year the sea breezes keep it delightfully cool for a tropical country. The soil is fertile and it was

1 The spelling of the name was originally Barbadoes, which has caused many persons to think that there was a group of islands of that name. The "e" was silent and in late years the name has come to be spelled as it has always been pronounced—Barbados with the principal accent on the second syllable.

the first English colony where sugar cane was planted. It is the most densely populated rural country in the world, China not excepted, the population averaging over 1,060 to the square mile.

George Washington visited this island with his invalid brother in 1751. It is the only country he ever visited outside of America. The history of the island has some significant features. It shows, for instance, the process of peaceful colonization accomplished without conquest or bloodshed. Its colonists have almost from the very beginning enjoyed representative institutions and the full measure of English freedom. The Church of England has always been the prevailing form of religion. The handsome and spacious church edifices in the various parishes as they exist today bear eloquent testimony to the hold which the Church of England has upon the inhabitants of this island. The foundation of the political organization of the community is the parish system brought from England in the seventeenth century, and preserved with less change than has taken place in the mother country. The island is divided into eleven parishes and the vestry is elected annually by the voters of the parish. The vestries are virtually municipal councils, which look after the maintenance of the public roads and poor relief, as well as the repair and maintenance of the churches.[2] At first the government of the island was proprietory, but in 1663 the Royal authority was established. The local government now consists of a governor, a legislative council, and the House of Assembly. The civil wars in England in Cromwell's times caused many to take refuge in this island, and the imprisonment and execution of Charles I induced others, many of whom had been officers of rank in the service of the King, to follow their example. In fact, during the first stages of the civil wars, Barbados had been an asylum for both the Royalists and the Parliamentarians, who sought to avoid the contest at home, and emigration to the island was very great. The emigration from the mother country, in fact, was so great during the commotions in England that in 1650, only 26 years after the

2 The same system obtained in South Carolina from the approval of the Church Act in 1706 to the disestablishment of the Church by the constitution of 1777-1778.

settlement of the island, it was computed that there were 20,000 white men in Barbados, half of them able to bear arms.[3] In 1670, Barbados could boast of 50,000 white and upwards of 100,000 black inhabitants, whose labors, it is said, gave employment to 60,000 tons of shipping. Upon the reestablishment of royal authority, Charles II honored thirteen gentlemen of Barbados with the dignity of baronetage, probably with the view to reward them for their loyalty and sufferings during the civil wars.

After the Spaniards had, in 1587, abandoned the plan of settling at Port Royal, little further was accomplished toward the permanent colonization of South Carolina for nearly a hundred years.[4] Charters and grants of land were, however, in this interval freely bestowed upon individuals and companies by the sovereigns of England, in other parts of America, and English colonies had been successfully established in Virginia in several parts of New England, and in Maryland. On October 30, 1629, Charles I, of England, granted to Sir. Robert Heath, his Attorney General, all of the territory of North America lying between the 31st and 36th parallels of north latitude and extending from the Atlantic to the Pacific, to be known as "Carolana, or Province of Carolana." Sir Robert did nothing toward settling his province and it was not until the second year after the restoration of Charles II that some of his adherents and courtiers, to whom he was indebted for distinguished services,

3 Bryan Edwards: *History of the West Indies*, 323.

4 Francisco Gordillo and Pedro de Quexos discovered the great harbor subsequently known as Port Royal on St. Helen's Day in 1521. It was thereafter known to the Spaniards as Santa Elena. Prior to 1562 several futile attempts were made by Spaniards to effect settlements there. In 1562 Jean Ribaut, a navigator sent by Coligny built a fort there on what is now Parris Island and garrisoned it with twenty-eight French Protestants and named it Charlesfort. The soldiers quarrelled among themselves, killed two of their number and finally built a crude boat and all but one of the survivors of them set sail for France about a year after their settlement. One young man refused to go with them, remaining with the Indians. Ribaut called this great harbor Port Royal. In 1564 the governor of Cuba sent Hernando Manrique de Rojas to Port Royal to destroy the French sett lement. He found that the settlers had left, but he destroyed their fort and captured Guillaume Roufli, the young man who had stayed behind.

In the spring of 1566 Pedro Menendez de Aveles, governor of Florida, planted a Spanish colony on the same island that the French had built their fort upon and built a larger and stronger fort than the French had had at another point on the island, and this they called San Felipe. Ten years later the Spaniards were driven out by the Indians, who destroyed San Felipe. In 1577 the Spaniards returned and built another fort one hundred and fifty feet from the site of Sail Felipe and made it impregnable to Indian attacks. This was called San Marcos. In 1587 San Marcos was abandoned, principally because the Spaniards realized that they could not defeat the encroachments of the English while carrying on a struggle with the Indians.

obtained a charter with extensive powers for the same territory, to be called Carolina instead of the earlier Carolana. This charter was dated March 24, 1662/3. It was a planter of Barbados, Sir John Colleton, who first suggested to Sir Anthony Ashley Cooper (Lord Ashley) that they, with associates, obtain a grant to this "rich and fertile Province of Carolina" from Charles II. The eight noblemen to whom this charter was granted were: Edward Hyde, Earl of Clarendon; George Monck, Duke of Albemarle; William, Lord Craven; John, Lord Berkeley; Anthony, Lord Ashley (afterwards Earl of Shaftesbury), Sir George Carteret, Sir William Berkeley, and Sir John Colleton. None of these proprietors was more active in the settlement of Carolina than Lord Ashley and none evinced more interest than he in the cause of the colonists. He was actively engaged in public affairs during the civil wars, first espousing the Royal cause and later that of Parliament, and finally aided in the Restoration. In 1672 he became Earl of Shaftesbury.

The first communication about the settlement of Carolina came from Sir John Colleton, a Barbadian, then in London. On June 10, 1663, he addressed a letter to the Duke of Albemarle stating that there were divers people that desired to settle and plant in the Province of Carolina and that one of the difficulties was the claim under a prior charter to Sir Robert Heath. Sir John Colleton was one of the thirteen gentlemen of Barbadoes upon whom Charles II had bestowed the dignity of baronetage. Another Barbadian gentlemen who subsequently received this dignity was Col. John Yeamans, who was created a baronet, January 12, 1664/5. These two names are intimately associated with the early settlement of Carolina.

Sir John Colleton had been a captain of foot and a most active partisan of royalty in the beginning of the civil wars. After the success of the Parliamentary forces he went to Barbados. There he still maintained the royal cause. He was the first of the Lords Proprietors to die. His death occurred in 1666.

Sir John Yeamans was the eldest son of John Yeamans, brewer of Bristol. He attained the rank of colonel in the royalist army and in about 1650 migrated to Barbados and engaged in planting. He was one of the council of that island from July 1660 to March 1664.

Light has been thrown upon the details of the settlement of Carolina and of the influences that set in motion the various expeditions, by the publication of the Shaftesbury papers. These were documents retained by the Earl of Shaftesbury (Lord Ashley), which passed from his successors down to the ninth Earl of Shaftesbury who died in 1886, after depositing them in the British Public Record Office. These papers make clear the important part that the Barbadians took in the settlement of Carolina and show the intimate connection between the inhabitants of Barbados and the early colonists of Carolina.[5]

While Sir John Colleton was seeking to remove the obstacle presented by claims under Sir Robert Heath's grant, Thomas Modyford, who had been governor of Barbados, and Peter Colleton, a son of Sir John Colleton, were preparing and submitting proposals for the settlement of a Barbadian colony in the province. This was doubtless because the planters of Barbados were becoming straitened for land. In the meantime, without waiting for the acceptance of their proposals, they sent out an expedition in the ship *Adventure,* under Captain William Hilton. Captain Hilton had previously made a voyage to the coast of what is now North Carolina. In consequence of reports received from him about the country near Charles (Cape Fear) River, a second expedition was organized under him to explore the coast of Carolina southward from Cape Fear to latitude 31° north. This expedition sailed from Speights Bay, Barbados, August 10, 1663.

On August 12, the "Adventurers," as the promoters of the expedition were called, addressed to the Lords Proprietors a petition requesting that the Barbadian adventurers, some two hundred in number, might be permitted to purchase from the Indians and hold under the Proprietors a tract of a thousand square miles in Carolina,

5 Numerous records of the provincial government of South Carolina now extant and being cared for and published by the Historical Commission of South Carolina sustain the showing of the Shaftesbury papers.

to be called the Corporation of the Barbadian Adventurers, and that they might have certain powers of self-government. The Proprietors answered on September 9, stating that their petition was referred to Colonel Modyford and Peter Colleton.

They reached the Carolina coast August 26, 1663, and explored the coast. On September 3, the expedition under Hilton entered the great harbor of Port Royal, having sailed from the Combahee River southward. He next sailed to Cape Fear and, after exploring the country in that vicinity, returned to Barbadoes. Upon his return, he and his associates wrote an account of their explorations. His *Relation* of his voyage and discoveries was published in London in 1664.[6] Hilton's name has been preserved in the nomenclature of a promontory at the mouth of Port Royal River known as Hilton Head[7] and by an island from which this head juts out known as Hilton Head Island.

The Proprietors, however, did not accept the proposals which had been submitted by those under whose auspices the expedition was made, and nothing came of this attempt at a settlement of the new province. The favorable account given by Hilton, as pointed out by Salley in *Narratives of Early Carolina,* 35, and the liberal inducements offered to settlers by the agents of the Proprietors, induced many settlers to go to South Carolina a few years later. Hilton's expedition, says the same writer, was of great assistance to the Lords Proprietors of Carolina in the work of settling the province and the publication of his account of his voyage induced hundreds of excellent people to settle in Carolina, as shown by the extant land grants. On 11 of January, 1665, Colonel John Yeamans received a commission as lieutenant general and governor of Carolina. The

6 A/ RELATION/ of / A Discovery lately made on the Coast of FLORIDA, / (From Lat. 31. to 33 Deg. 45 Min. North-Lat.) / By William Hilton Commander, and / Commissioner with Capt. Anthony Long, and / Peter Fabian, in the Ship Adventure, which set Sayl / from Spikes Bay, Aug. 10, 1663. and was set / forth by several Gentlemen and Merchants / of the Island of Barbadoes. / Giving an account of the nature and temperature of the / Soyl, the manners and disposition of the Natives, and whatsoever / else is remarkable therein. / Together with / Proposals made by the Commissioners of / the Lords Proprietors, to all such persons as shall / become the first Setlers on the Rivers, Harbors, / and Creeks there. / London, / Printed by J. C. for Simon Miller / at the Star neer the West-end of St. Pauls, / 1664.

7 This point was discovered by Gordillo and Quexos in 1521 and called by them Punta de Santa Elena.

Proprietors had received a good report of his abilities and loyalty and they had induced the King, as above stated, to confer the honor of a Knight Baronet upon him and his heirs. Under this commission, Sir John Yeamans organized an expedition to explore the lower coast of Carolina to select a proper site. These "Adventurers," as they were called, not only wanted Carolina opened up to settlers, but believed that settlers in Carolina could there produce "wines, currents, raisins, silks, etc., the planting of which will not injure other Plantations, which may very well happen if there were a very great increase of sugar works or more tobacco, ginger, cotton and indigo made than the world will vent."[8]

Those engaged in the venture were to be entitled to 500 acres of land for every 1,000 pounds of Muscovado sugar contributed. The expedition consisting of a fly boat, a frigate and a sloop, set out from Barbados and reached the Charles (Cape Fear) River. In attempting to enter the river without a pilot, the fly boat was stranded and destroyed.

Governor Yeamans found the settlers at Charles River in such needy condition that he sent the sloop to Virginia to secure provisions for them, and he returned to Barbados in the frigate. He left Lieutenant Colonel Robert Sandford, Secretary of the Province, to carry out the explorations. Sandford proceeded with his explorations along the coast of Carolina. He has left an admirable account of his voyage. In his quaint style he describes the country that opened up to his view, with its vast expanse of green marsh resembling a rich prarie, its broad and noble arms of the sea, rivers, and innumerable creeks fringed with oak and cedar and myrtle and jessamine,[9] all so familiar to those who have ever seen the Carolina coast. One of the places he visited was Port Royal and among the Indians who came to see him was a Cassique of the country of Kiawah, who urged him to go to his country, assuring him of a broad and deep entrance and promising a large welcome and plentiful entertainment and trade. Sandford

8 *State Papers, Colonial, 1661–68.*

9 The yellow jessamine of the South is an entirely different plant from the common jasmine of other climes. See Porcher's *Resources of the Southern Fields and Forests.*

proceeded with his explorations, taking the Indian for a pilot, and finally found himself before the river that led into the country of Kiawah. He did not make a landing, though he was persuaded that it was an excellent country. He called the river Ashley in compliment to Lord Ashley.

Sandford, having concluded his voyage, returned to the Charles River, but the Barbadian settlement there[10] was finally broken up and abandoned in the summer or fall of 1667. Thus it was the Barbadian planters who first took up the project of establishing the settlement on the Cape Fear River.

In the meantime, the Proprietors took the first steps to formulate a government for the great province they were to found. Under the leadership of Lord Ashley, not yet the Earl of Shaftesbury, John Locke, the celebrated philosopher, prepared the famous "Fundamental Constitutions" for the government of Carolina, which were formally adopted by the Proprietors in July 1669. This was an extraordinary scheme of forming an aristocratic government of a colony of adventurers in the wild woods, among savages and wild beasts. One of the reasons given for these constitutions was "that the government of the Province may be made most agreeable to the Monarchy under which we live and of which this Province is a part, *and that we may avoid erecting a numerous democracy."* The charter constituted the province a *County Palatine.* The first clause of the constitution accordingly provided that the eldest of the Lords Proprietors should be the Palatine (that is, the Governor with the privileges of vice-royalty) and upon his decease the eldest of the seven surviving Proprietors should always succeed him.[11] There were to be two orders of nobility besides the Proprietors, namely, Landgraves and Cassiques. Each county was to contain 480,000 acres. The eight Proprietors were each to have 96,000 acres. There were to be as many Landgraves as counties and twice as many Cassiques. Each Landgrave was to have 48,000 acres and each Cassique, 24,000 acres. This left three-fifths of each county or 288,000 acres for the people. McCrady says that this body of laws never received

10 Called Charles Town.

11 *Statutes at Large of South Carolina,* I, 42.

the necessary assent and approbation of the freemen of the province, and so was never constitutionally of force, but its provisions had an effect upon the institutions of the province and an influence upon the customs and habits of the people.[12] By the constitutions, the eldest of the Lords Proprietors, who should personally be present in Carolina, was thereby in fact the deputy of the Palatine, and if no Proprietor nor heir apparent of a Proprietor was in Carolina, then the Palatine should choose for deputy any one of the Landgraves who should be in the province. It was probably to meet the provisions of the constitutions, as has been pointed out, that one third of the governors appointed by the Proprietors were made Landgraves, and thus each became, while serving as governor, deputy of the Palatine.[13] The plan provided for a Grand Council and for a parliament. The Grand Council, among other duties, were to prepare all matters to be introduced in Parliament,

12 McCrady: *South Carolina Under the Proprietary Government,* 110. These Constitutions were, however, not rejected by the people, as most historians assert, but were superseded from time to time by "instructions" from the Proprietors to the governors. The Proprietors were awaiting development before attempting to carryout the plans of the Constitutions and, as the province advanced, many of the provisions were successfully inaugurated and quiescently followed.

13 Two thirds of the Proprietary governors were never made landgraves. Colonel William Sayle, the first governor of South Carolina, was never made a landgrave, possibly because he did not live long enough. Robert Quary was elected governor by the Grand Council and the Proprietors refused to sanction the election and so he was not made a landgrave. Philip Ludwell, who was appointed by the Proprietors, was not made a landgrave. Joseph Blake, who was elected governor by the Grand Council upon the death of Landgrave Smith in November, 1694, appears never to have been made a landgrave by the Proprietors. Landgrave Smith, evidently to give him the title of landgrave that he might receive the preferential vote due to a landgrave by the Grand Council, willed him his title of landgrave. When Governor Archdale retired in 1696 he appointed Blake deputy governor, as provided by the Constitutions. At the same time he induced his son Thomas Archdale to sell his proprietorship to Governor Blake in order that his title to the governorship might be perfectly clear, under the provision of the Constitutions that a Proprietor in the province could assume the governorship as vice-palatine, or deputy of the palatine. Blake then quit claim to the landgravate that had been willed to him by Smith. Governor Archdale himself, acting as a Proprietor in behalf of his minor son, had been selected by the Proprietors, but was never made a landgrave. James Moore, who was elected by the Grand Council in September, 1700, to succeed Blake, was never made a landgrave although he served to March, 1703. Col. Edward Tynte, who was commissioned governor of North and South Carolina, December 9, 1708, was never made a landgrave. He did not arrive in Charles Town and assume the governorship until November 26, 1709, and he died June 20, 1710. Charles Craven, although the brother of a Proprietor and sometime Palatine, was never made a landgrave although he served six years as governor. His successor, Col. Robert Johnson, was never made a landgrave. Robert Gibbes who was elected governor by the Grand Council, upon the death of Tynte in 1710 was not approved of by the Proprietors and was not made a landgrave. Robert Daniell, who was appointed deputy governor by Governor Craven upon his departure from the province in 1716, was already a landgrave. Thus we see that of the eighteen men who served as governors under the Proprietors eleven were not landgraves, and of the twelve appointed by the Proprietors five were never landgraves. Sothell, Archdale and Blake were Proprietors. Quary, Moore and Gibbes were named by the Grand Council and were not commissioned by the Proprietors. Sayle, Ludwell, Tynte, Craven and Robert Johnson were Proprietors's appointees who were not made landgraves. Yeamans, West, Morton, Kyrle, Colleton, Smith and Sir Nathaniel Johnson were appointees by the Proprietors who were made landgraves.

and controversies of a certain character were to be determined by them. The freeholders were to meet to choose a parliament. It was an elaborate scheme of government worked out for the province that was sought to be established.

The Proprietors had already turned their attention to plans of colonization. The failure of the settlement at Cape Fear and the glowing account which Sandford had given of the country at Port Royal in his *Relation,* published in 1666, induced the Proprietors to turn their attention to that part of the coast of Carolina. The next attempt at colonization was an expedition under Joseph West. On the 27th of July, 1669, he was commissioned by the Lords Proprietors commander-in-Chief of a fleet of three vessels which was to transport the very first settlers that were to take possession of the province of Carolina. The expedition was to go by way of Barbados and West's commandership was to continue only until the fleet arrived at Barbados. Sir John Yeamans, although still active in the political affairs of Barbadoes, still bore the commission of lieutenant general and governor of Carolina. There appears a commission from the Lords Proprietors, dated July 26, 1669, appointing William Sayle governor of the province of Carolina. This commission was originally issued with a blank space for the name and was intended either for Sir John Yeamans, then in Barbados, or for such person as should be selected by him. The fleet, consisting of three vessels, under West's command, encountered a storm at Barbados and the *Albemarle* was wrecked. A sloop was procured at Barbados to take its place. Sir John Yeamans took command of the fleet and the voyage for Carolina was resumed at the end of November. About the middle of December the fleet was scattered by hurricanes, near the island of Nevis. The *Port Royal* was wrecked on the Bahamas and the Barbadian sloop was driven to Virginia. The *Carolina* reached Bermuda January 12, 1669/70. There Sir John Yeamans, exercising the discretionary powers given him, filled in the blank commission for a governor with the name of Col. William Sayle, who took command of the expedition, and sailed for Carolina after procuring a sloop to replace the *Port Royal.* Yeamans returned to Barbados. The *Carolina* reached what is now Bull's Island, March 15, and Port Royal, March 21.

The foregoing account shows that the first governor of South Carolina was accidentally appointed. The reason given for his appointment was that being a Bermudian it was thought that that might be an inducement to others in Bermuda to settle in South Carolina. The first landing of this expedition was made March 16, 1669/70, at Seewee Bay at the back of Onisecaw, which was later called Bull's Island. The Cassique of Kiawah, presumably the same who had tried to persuade Sandford to visit the country of Kiawah, now again came to the ships and repeated the favorable accounts that had been given of his country. Taking the Indian with them, they sailed for Port Royal, where they made a short stay. However, no settlement as such was made at Port Royal. There is no evidence that a single article, either implement or supplies, was ever landed there from the ships. During their short stay at Port Royal, Governor Sayle summoned the "freemen," according to the instructions accompanying his commission, to elect five men "to be of the council," and they elected Paul Smith, Robert Donne, Ralph Marshall, Samuel West and Joseph Dalton as their representatives. This was the first election in South Carolina. There is no record whether it was by ballot or by poll. The expedition then left Port Royal upon the arrival of the sloop procurred at Bermuda and, after a stop at St. Helena and after much discussion, it was determined to favor the Kiawah country, and the vessels stood to the north and entered the waters forming what is now Charleston Harbor. The colonists landed from the *Carolina* and the Bermudan sloop early in April 1670, in the country of Kiawah on the west bank of the river which Sandford, in passing, had named the Ashley. The sloop which had been secured at Barbadoes to take the place of the *Albermarle* arrived at Kiawah May 23, 1670, and from time to time within the next year the colonists were increased by the arrival of some Barbadian planters and their servants and negro slaves. The point on which they settled they named Albermarle Point. So it appears that an Indian chief, the Cassique of Kiawah, is responsible for the final location on the Ashley. In *Narratives of Early Carolina,* A.S. Salley, Jr., states that the pride which the Cassique of Kiawah took in his harbor and his country was responsible for the settling there of the first English colony in South Carolina, and he adds that the "same pardonable pride in the place is still characteristic of the inhabitants of the Kiawah country." Thus did the first settlers arrive in Carolina. Two of the three ships that sailed from England and some lives had been lost. Just how many of the original company arrived at Kiawah cannot now be ascertained. The company had been increased at Kinsale and Barbados, and some also had probably joined at Bermuda, and Dr. Henry Woodward joined at Nevis. Only one ship, the *Carolina,* out of the original expedition reached South Carolina. Five had been engaged in the expedition from the time the colonists left England to the landing at Kiawah.

The settlement grew but slowly. Governor Sayle's health soon failed. He was authorized by his commission, with the advice of the Grand Council, to nominate a deputy to succeed him in case he should die. A few hours before his death he called the Council and nominated Joseph West to be his successor. The Council met the afternoon after his death and elected West, March 4, 1670. The Proprietors confirmed West's selection. As early as 1670, Lord Ashley wrote to West that he was to take notice that Ashley River had been so named by Sandford, and was still to be so called, and that the town as planted out was to be called Charles Town, but it was not until September 1, 1671, that the name appears to have been adopted. During the Proprietory Government, the name of the town was written *Charles Town.* Upon the incorporation of the town, August 13, 1783, the name was changed to Charleston.

Sir John Yeamans arrived in Carolina some time in 1671 and settled on the point formed by the junction of Wappoo Creek and Ashley River. He became prominent in the affairs of the province. He received, April 5, 1671, the title of landgrave from the Lords Proprietors, being the first inhabitant of the province to receive that title. He was sent a commission as governor by the Proprietors, and superceded West on the 19th of April, 1672. In the letter accompanying the commission, Lord Ashley recommended to him to make another port town on the Ashley. The present was too low. He must lay out the great port town into regular streets. Governor Yeamans and the Grand Council on April 30th directed John Culpeper, the Surveyor General, to lay out a new town at Oyster Point. The town thus laid out extended no farther west than the present Meeting Street, nor farther north than Broad Street, nor south than Water Street. Governor Yeamans served until August 1674, but seems to have "lost out" with the Proprietors because of his championship of the infant settlement and his urgency that greater support should be extended and larger supplies sent to it than the Proprietors, who were more impatient for returns than desirous of further expenditures, were willing to accede to.[14] Dr. Alexander Hewat, whose *Historical Account of South Carolina* was published in 1799, says: "About the year 1674 Sir John Yeamans, being reduced to a feeble and sickly condition by the warm climate and his indefatigable labors for the success of the settlement, returned to Barbadoes, where he died."[15] This is an erroneous statement. The error has been repeated by Ramsay and Simms and even by such careful historians as Rivers and McCrady. The first person to call attention to the error was Mr. Langdon Cheves, the editor of the Shaftesbury papers.[16] The fact is that he died in South Carolina in August, 1674, probably upon the plantation on Wappoo Creek, its junction with Ashley River, for there when he was governor of the province in 1672-1674, he had a "countrey house," palisaded and garrisoned by his negroes. Another error touching Sir John Yeamans is as to the marriage of his widow, Lady Margaret. It has been stated that she married Governor James Moore. The fact is that Governor Moore married Margaret Berringer, the daughter of Lady Margaret Yeamans, widow of Sir John Yeamans, by a former husband, Lt. Col. Benjamin Berringer. It has been claimed that Yeamans' "Yeamans Hall" on Goose Creek was the "countrey house" which Sir John Yeamans built when

14 This *Magazine*, 152–156.

15 B.R. Carroll: *Historical Collections of South Carolina*, I, 70.

16 *Collections of the South Carolina Historical Society*, V, 452.

he came into the province, and to which he retired when the people would not "salute him governor," though he was a landgrave. This claim lacks confirmation and it is improbable that he ever resided upon this property, which long belonged to the family of Thomas Smith, the second landgrave of that name.[17] The widow of Sir John Yeamans married the third time William Walley, whether in Barbadoes or South Carolina is not known.[18]

Upon the death of Sir John Yeamans in the Province early in August 1674, Joseph West was again elected Governor by the Grand Council, August 13th, to which position he had by the Proprietors already, by an as yet undelivered commission of May 1674, been appointed. In his whole career in the province, Governor West seems to have preserved the esteem and confidence both of the Proprietors and the people and to have administered the trusts confided to him honestly, skillfully, and successfully. He served as governor three times in all over ten years.

South Carolina was continually receiving additions in those early days from Barbadoes and the other West India islands. The course of communication between South Carolina and England continued for many years to be principally by way of Barbadoes, and, as has been already stated, the first colony sent by the Proprietors to South Carolina was consigned to agents there, being thence dispatched to South Carolina. The Barbadians who came to South Carolina were all Church of England people and formed a great part of the church party in the province. Besides Sir John Yeamans, there came from that island Sir John Colleton's son James, the governor, in1686, and his grandson, Major Charles Colleton. From that island also came Captain John Godfrey, sometime a deputy and member of the Grand Council; Christopher Portman, John Maverick, and Thomas Gray, among the first members of the Grand Council; Captain Gyles Hall, one of the first settlers, and an owner of a lot in old Charles Town; Robert Daniell, landgrave and governor; Arthur and Edward Middleton; Benjamin Gibbes, and Robert Gibbes, afterwards governor; Barnard

17 This *Magazine*, XIX, 69.

18 *Journal of the Grand Council*, 1672-1680, p. 81.

Schenckingh, who was appointed by the Grand Council high sheriff for Berkeley County and chief judge of the province; Charles Butler, Robert Dearsley, and Alexander Skene. Among others from Barbadoes were those of the following names, many eminent in South Carolina history, namely: Drayton, Beresford, Elliott, Fenwicke, Foster, Fox, Gibbon, Hare, Hayden, Lake, Ladson, Moore, Strode, Thompson, Walter, and Woodward.

Generally speaking, the Barbadian and the English colonists settled in Charles Town and upon the Cooper and Ashley Rivers; the French Huguenots on the Santee, at the Orange Quarter on the Eastern Branch of Cooper River and in Charles Town; and the English Dissenters, who had come over with Morton, Blake, Axtell and the Scotch Dissenters Lord Cardross, upon the Edisto. Berkeley County was thus for the Church of England, Colleton was strongly imbued with dissent, and Craven, while Calvinistic in its tenets, was without hostility to the church.[19]

The Barbadian element exercised an appreciable influence upon the development of society in South Carolina. In the other colonies of America, society was built up upon the various influences which surrounded it in its growth and development but, as has been suggested, many of the earliest settlers in South Carolina, coming from Barbadoes, where a colonial society was already fully developed, brought with them customs and precedents upon which that of South Carolina was formed. The social order in Barbadoes was based upon African slavery. Those who came to South Carolina from Barbadoes brought their slaves with them. Oldmixon tells us that the gentlemen of Barbadoes lived like sovereigns on their plantations; they had their servants of the household and those of the field; their tables were spread every day with a variety of nice dishes, and their attendants were more numerous than many of the nobility in England, their equipages were rich, their liveries fine, their coaches and horse the same; their chairs, chaises, and all the conveniences of their traveling, magnificent. Their dress and that of their ladies was fashionable and costly, and having been bred in London,

19 *McCrady: South Carolina under Proprietary Government,* 329.

their behavior was genteel and polite; in which way, says the author, they had the advantage of most of the country gentlemen of England, who, living at a distance from London, frequent the world very little, and from conversing always with their dogs, horses and rude peasants, acquire an air suitable to their society. The gentlemen of Barbadoes were civil, generous, hospitable, and very sociable. "In short," says the same author, "the inhabitants of Barbadoes live as plentifully and some of them as luxuriously as any in the world. They have everything that is requisite for pomp and luxury; they are absolute lords of all things—life and limb of their servants excepted—within their own territory, and some of them have no less than 700 or 800 negroes, who are themselves and their posterity their slaves forever." Such a description might as well apply to the coast country of South Carolina in *ante bellum* days. Lawson's description of Carolina contemporary with that of Oldmixon, corresponds in a remarkable degree. The merchants of Carolina, says Lawson, are fair and frank traders. The gentlemen seated in the country are very courteous, live very nobly in their houses, and give very genteel entertainments to all strangers and others that come to visit them. The main features of the slave code brought over by the Barbadians were adopted in South Carolina. The scheme of the court of justices and freeholders was taken from the Barbadian Act. The churchmen who settled Barbadoes established parishes, adding civil to the ecclesiastical duties of parochial officers. The same system was accepted in South Carolina. The Church Act of 1706 adopted in South Carolina the names of many of the parished of Baradoes, to-wit: St. Michael's, St. Thomas's, St. John's, Christ Church, St. James's, St. Phillip's, St. Andrew's and St. George's, and following the custom in Barbadoes, the church wardens and vestry were invested with many civil as well as ecclesiastical duties. The love of the South Carolina gentleman for his gun and dog and horse and his devotion to all field sports doubtless is an inherited instinct traceable to his English descent.

The system of government brought from Barbados by the early settlers was imbued with the military spirit, so much so that the high sheriff of the province retained the military title of "provost-marshal" for a hundred years—indeed until the American Revolution. Under this system the province, and afterwards the state, was divided into military districts; the chief of each was a colonel, and these again in other districts, or beats, under captains. As the duties were onerous the office was not usually held longer than the term. So each young man of prominence took his term of duty, and thus acquiring the title of captain retained it unless he became a colonel. There were usually, therefore, a considerable number of men in each community having the title of "captain" or "colonel." To this source may be traced the prevalence of military titles in South Carolina. The English custom of giving individual names to places where one locates doubtless was introduced into South Carolina by the settlers that came from Barbados. It is a pleasing fact to note that in 1766, nearly 100 years after the Barbadians came to South Carolina, the South Carolina legislature graciously voted £785 for the relief of those who suffered in Barbados in that year from a dreadful fire.

Barbados is the only British possession with a charter which secures for Barbadians the independence of their legislative assembly. It is a self-governing commonwealth, and Barbadians have ever been proud of their ancient rights and privileges. Who can say how much of the conservatism of old South Carolina, how much of the ancient pride of the people in the laws and institutions of their State, was due to the influence of the Barbadian element, so largely predominant in the early history of South Carolina?

> Custom forms us all:
> Our thoughts, our morals, our most fixed beliefs,
> Are consequences of our place of birth.

Barbados is so thoroughly English that it has been called "Little England." When one looks at the map of this island and reads the names of the ancient parishes, St. Michael's, St. Phillip's, Christ Church, St. John's, St. Thomas's, St. James's, St. Andrew's and St. Peter's, he feels that he must be in lower South Carolina, for there he finds parishes with identical names. If he were to go today to that island he would land at Bridgetown in the harbor in Carlisle Bay, and would first put his feet upon *Bay Street.* From thence he would walk to *Broad Street,* the principal street of the town, upon which he would find the public buildings, respectable in their old age. From thence he would enter the precincts of old St. Michael's Church, dating back to the 17th century, the pride and ornament of the town, with its stone paved floors, with its monuments set in the floors, and with its memorials upon its walls commemorating its sainted and honored dead. He would continue his walk in the old residential section of the town. He would find high walls enclosing the dwelling houses and through the iron grilled gates he would get a peep of beautiful gardens, and as the perfume of fragrant flowers was wafted to him upon the gentle breeze, he would feel that he breathes a familiar atmosphere; and though nearly two hundred and fifty years have elapsed since the first Barbadians helped to settle South Carolina and to build old Charles Town, he would know that the traditions and customs of old England reached South Carolina soil in large measure through the island of Barbados, and that it was the Barbadians who gave character to the early social and political structure of South Carolina.[20]

20 It may add to the interest of the article if the names of some of the earlier settlers from Barbados are given here. Of course, there were many more of whom no record remains.

LIST: Sir John Yeamans (S.C. Historical Society Collections, Vol. S, p. 52); Dr. Henry Woodward (The first English settler in S.C.,This Mag., Vol. 8, p. 33); Arthur Middleton (This Mag., Vol. 1, p. 229); Thomas and Robert Gibbes (This Mag., Vol. 12, p. 79); The Colletons (This Mag., Vol. 1, p. 327); Miles Brewton (Vol. 2, p. 128); John Culpeper (S.C. Col., Vol. 5, p. 285); Bernard Schenckingh (This Mag., Vol. 4, p. 239); George Bedon (S.C. Hist. Col., Vol. 5, p. 358); Col. John Godfrey and servants (ibid., p.30); Hugh Carteret (or Cartwright), (ibid., p. 396); Maurice Mathews (ibid., p. 332); The Canteys (This Mag., Vol. 11, p. 203); The Draytons (T his Mag., Vol. 14, p. 16); Richard Tookerman (Will of wife Catharine, Probate Court Book, 10, p. 231); George Thompson (S.C. Col., Vol. 5, p. 30);. James Moore (ibid., p. 463); William Murrell (ibid., p. 426); Samuel Lucas (ibid., p. 425); Joseph Pendarvis (ibid., p. 418); Original Jackson ibid., 410); Sam Boswood (ibid., p. 271); Joan Burnet (ibid.); John Cole (ibid.); Moses Flower (ibid.); Enoch Howell (ibid.); Thomas Patt ison (ibid.); Richard Poore (ibid.); John Ratcliff (ibid.); Thomas Witty (ibid.) ; John Robinson (ibid.); Joseph Dowden (ibid.); Thomas Finden (ibid.) ; Thomas Holton and servants (ibid.); Philip Comerten (ibid.); James Donohoe (ibid.); John Faulconer (ibid.); John Norton (ibid.); James Needham (ibid.); Edward Roberts (ibid.); Oliver Spencer (ibid.); Thomas Thomson (ibid.); Henry Wood (ibid.); John Pinke also servants (ibid.); B. Fitzpatrick (ibid.); John Griffin (ibid.); John Foster (ibid.); Capt. Gyles Hall (ibid.); Mr. Christopher Portman (ibid.); 42 men, women and children came on ship John and Thomas including Mr. John Maverick and servants, Philip Jones, Richard Rowser (ibid.); 64 immigrants were said to have come on Carolina (ibid. p. 382); and 20 more by the Charles (ibid.); It is said also in certain *memoranda* in the handwriting of John Locke (ibid., p. 252) that 80 people were going from Barbadoes to Carolina and possibly more. Whether the names we have given are included in these figures cannot be known now. We give also the following names: Christopher Berrow and wife (ibid., p. 137); H. Hughes (ibid.); Thomas Norris (ibid.); John Jones (ibid.); H. Symonds (ibid.); J. Collins (ibid.); James Marshall (ibid.); A. Churne (ibid.); William Carr (ibid.); James Gilbert (ibid., p. 237); Hugh Strode (ibid., p. 243) and about 30 with Yeamans (ibid., 382).

The English Sugar Islands and the Founding of South Carolina

RICHARD S. DUNN

RICHARD S. DUNN IS PROFESSOR OF HISTORY AT THE UNIVERSITY OF PENNSYLVANIA, PHILADELPHIA. THIS PAPER WAS PRESENTED AT THE SOUTH CAROLINA TRICENTENNIAL SYMPOSIUM, MARCH 19, 1970, IN COLUMBIA, S.C.

Originally published in Volume 72, Number 2 (April 1971)

Everyone who has examined the founding of South Carolina agrees that planters from the West Indies played a major role—some would say a decisive role—in shaping the new colony. The most recent historian of colonial South Carolina, Eugene Sirmans, argues that settlers from Barbados, congregating at Goose Creek a few miles above Charleston, formed the dominant political faction in the first generation of settlement. Sirmans labels the opening section of his book, spanning the years from 1670 to 1712, the age of the Goose Creek men.[1]

Sirmans may exaggerate the prominence of West Indians in early Carolina, but not by much. Agnes Baldwin has just published a list of 684 settlers who came to Carolina between 1670 and 1680. In this list, half the settlers whose place of origin she can identify came from the West Indies.[2] And if we examine the backgrounds of the governors of South Carolina between 1669 and 1737, it turns out that nearly half—eleven out of twenty-three—had lived in the islands or were sons of islanders. Seven of the early Carolina governors had Barbados backgrounds.[3] Hence the Goose Creek men are indeed crucial to our understanding of early South Carolina.

1 M. Eugene Sirmans, *Colonial South Carolina*, 1663-1763 (Chapel Hill, 1966), pp. 19-100. See also J.P. Thomas, "The Barbadians in Early South Carolina," *South Carolina Historical and Genealogical Magazine*, XXXI (1930), 75-92; Edward McCrady, *History of South Carolina under the Proprietary Government, 1670-1719* (New York, 1897), ch. 3, 5-8; C. M. Andrews, *The Colonial Period of American History* (4 vols. New Haven, 1934-1938), III, ch. 5; W.F. Craven, *The Southern Colonies in the Seventeenth Century, 1607-1689* (Baton Rouge, 1949), ch. 9.

2 Agnes Leland Baldwin, *First Settlers of South Carolina, 1670-1680* (Columbia, S.C., 1969). She lists 146 who came from the island colonies, 134 from Britain, and 10 from the mainland colonies. The remaining 394 she assigns no place of origin; 8 or 10 of these, at least, I can pretty certainly identify as coming from Barbados.

3 Jack P. Greene, *The Quest for Power* (Chapel Hill, 1963) lists the South Carolina governors and assembly leaders, pp. 457-458, 475-488. Governors who came from the islands, or whose fathers came from the islands, were William Sayle (Bermuda), Sir John Yeamans (Barbados), James Colleton (Barbados), James Moore (Barbados), Sir Nathaniel Johnson (Leeward Islands), Robert Gibbes (Barbados), Robert Daniel (Barbados), Robert Johnson (Leeward Islands), James Moore, Jr. (Barbados), Arthur Middleton (Barbados) and Thomas Broughton (Leeward Islands).

Who were these Goose Creek men? Why did they leave the Caribbean islands at a time when the sugar industry was booming there, in order to face unknown challenges in the Carolina wilderness? What sort of colonizing expertise did they bring with them from the island colonies? And what social habits did they introduce to Carolina? Such questions have hitherto gone unasked and unanswered, because no one has examined the social structure of the English sugar islands in the late seventeenth century. Now a number of scholars are exploring aspects of Caribbean history which bear directly upon the founding of South Carolina. Many puzzles remain. But I believe that a social analysis of Barbados and Jamaica, circa 1670, does tell us something about the Goose Creek men and the thrust they imparted to South Carolina.

In 1670, the several English island colonies were at quite different stages of development. Barbados was the richest, most highly developed, most populous, and most congested English colony in America, with a thriving sugar industry and 50,000 inhabitants, including 30,000 Negroes. The Leeward Islands of St. Kitts, Nevis, Antigua and Montserrat were considerably less prosperous and well settled than Barbados, though by mainland standards they were very crowded and intensively cultivated. In these four islands the sugar industry was not yet fully developed; most of the Leeward planters were still small farmers with few or no slaves. Jamaica, a far larger place than Barbados or the Leewards, and potentially the most valuble English sugar producer, was in 1670 a raw and boisterous frontier outpost, best known as a buccaneer's lair. The Jamaican sugar industry was growing fast, but most of the land on the island was still untamed jungle. In Bermuda and the Bahamas, by contrast, there was little potential for further growth. Both of these island groups were economically stunted, for they lay too far north for sugar production. Bermuda—the oldest and smallest English colony—was an overcrowded, isolated, bucolic community of small tobacco farmers and fishermen. The Bahaman archipelago sheltered a few squatters who cut braziletto wood and gathered ambergris.

Settlers were drawn to South Carolina from all of these islands during the late seventeenth century. The tie with the Bahamas was especially close, since the Carolina proprietors also governed these islands, or tried to. The Earl of Shaftesbury ordered the ragged island squatters to adopt his pet institutional scheme, the Fundamental Constitutions, but his effort to staff the Bahaman Grand Council with titled manor lords failed even more spectacularly than in South Carolina.

Jamaica was of course some distance removed from Carolina, but it sent a number of settlers, including Thomas Pinckney, founder of a famous family, who arrived in 1692 on a Jamaican privateer. Mrs. Baldwin has not been able to uncover many recruits from the Leeward Islands, but I suspect there were a good number. The most notable early arrival from these islands was Sir Nathaniel Johnson, the Jacobite governor of the Leeward Islands, who fled to Carolina after the Glorious Revolution with his gang of 100 slaves and later became governor of South Carolina. But the principal Caribbean migration came from the most distant English island—Barbados.

It was a Barbados planter, Sir John Colleton, who first organized the proprietary group which received a royal charter from Charles II in 1663. Three boatloads of colonists from Barbados tried to plant at Cape Fear from 1665 to 1667, and about twenty Barbadians joined the first permanent South Carolina settlement on the Ashley River in 1670. During the decade of the 1670s, some 175 Barbadians can be identified as coming to the new colony. They brought with them at least 150 servants and slaves. This migration to Carolina was part of a general exodus from the overcrowded little island. One historian reckons that 30,000 white persons moved from Barbados to the other English mainland and island colonies in the thirty years between 1650 and 1680.[4] Such an estimate is certainly inflated. The total out—migration from Barbados during the entire seventeenth century was more likely 10,000—which is still sizable enough! South Carolina was by *no* means the chief destination for these migrants. In 1679, for instance, at the height of the Carolina migration, 593 white persons obtained tickets to leave Barbados; only thirty-eight of these people sailed to the Carolinas, many fewer than that went to New England or Virginia.[5] But the migration to Carolina was important, nonetheless, because many of the Barbados recruits were people of exceptional energy, experience and wealth.

It is often said that the people who quit Barbados and the other sugar islands were misfits and failures, poor whites who had not done well in the Caribbean, small planters squeezed off their farms by the aggressive big planters, and wage workers unable to compete with black slave labor. I think this picture is distorted at best. In Agnes Baldwin's list, we find a medley of rich and poor colonists moving from the islands to Carolina,

4 Alfred D. Chandler, "The Expansion of Barbados," *Journal of the Barbados Museum and Historical Society*, XIII (1945-46), 106.

5 Richard S. Dunn, "The Barbados Census of 1680: Profile of the Richest Colony in English America," *William and Mary Quarterly*, 3d ser., XXVI (1969), 26-28.

a cross section of big and middling sugar planters, merchants, artisans, small farmers, sailors, servants and slaves. To me, the most striking thing is the number of persons of wealth and position who chose to come. And it is also striking to find how many poor whites did *not* leave. Here, the Barbados census of 1680 is an extraordinarily illuminating document. It shows that many thousand poor whites still hung on in Barbados, despite thirty years of out-migration. The great majority of Barbados landholders in 1680 were very small farmers who held a few acres of inferior land and a few slaves apiece. These people were as repressed and voiceless as the submerged laboring class in England. Richard Ligon has a vivid description of the miserable way they lived in Barbados back around 1650, toiling in the sun all day, eating a meager diet of cassava bread, corn meal mush, and salt meat, and cooped up in low-roofed and windowless little houses "like Stoves, or heated Ovens." The Barbados poor whites, he says, were so depressed and sluggish that they lacked the enterprise to open their houses to the refreshing breeze and make themselves comfortable.[6] Such people cannot have been much better off in 1680. They had every reason to leave. But evidently many did not have the gumption to pick up and move to Carolina.

In mid-century Barbados, one of the most progressive-minded planters was a gentleman named Captain Benjamin Middleton. Richard Ligon designed an airy, shady home for him. Two of the captain's sons, Edward and Arthur, moved to South Carolina in the 1670s and launched a great Carolina dynasty. The Middletons were members of the Barbados ruling caste, the inner circle of some 175 big sugar planters with 60 or more slaves apiece, who held the best land, sold the most sugar, and monopolized the chief offices on the island. Big planters like the Middletons enjoyed privileges in Barbados more tangible than the aristocratic trappings dreamed up by Shaftesbury and Locke in the Fundamental Constitutions of Carolina. Yet we find that representatives from at least eighteen of these preeminent families obtained extensive land grants in South Carolina between 1672 and 1692.[7] Additional Carolina grants went to members of

6 Ibid., pp. 8, 12, 16-17; Richard Ligon, A True and Exact History of the Island of Barbados (London, 1657), pp. 40-43.

7 The eighteen families I can identify with some certainty are Berringer, Clutterbuck, Colleton, Davies, Dowden, Elliott, Fenwick, Foster, Gibbes, Hall, Lane, Lake, Merrick, Middleton. Quintyne, Robinson, Sandford and Yeamans. I have correlated the names of the 175 big planters in the Barbados census of 1680 with the names in Baldwin, *First Settlers of South Carolina* and A.S. Salley, ed., *Warrants for Lands in South Carolina, 1672-1692* (Columbia, S.C., 1910, 1915).

the lesser Barbados gentry, sugar planters with 20 to 60 slaves. Why should these people, who were making more money in the Indies than any North American planters or merchants, be willing to invest in an untracked wilderness 1,500 miles away? After all, the chief Virginia tobacco planters in 1670 took little or no interest in South Carolina.

The explanation, I think, is that the Barbados sugar planters needed fresh avenues for their younger children. They had no expansion room on Barbados. All of the choice land on the island was already partitioned into efficiently sized plantations by 1670, and the marginal land which they did not want in any case—was all held by the poor whites. In the case of the Middletons, they tried to start new sugar estates in Antigua, and lost heart when the French plundered this island in the 1660s. So Edward and Arthur came to Carolina. These brothers were younger sons. Their elder brother Benjamin stayed in Barbados and operated the main family estate with its 379 acres and 130 slaves, which doubtless remained more valuable for many years than Edward's new plantation called "The Oaks" on Goose Creek.

Not all of the leading Barbados families prospered in South Carolina. Take, for example, the Colletons. Like the Middletons, the Colletons were big Barbados planters who developed extensive interests in South Carolina. Sir John Colleton had been the prime organizer of the Carolina proprietorship. In the 1670s and 1680s, his eldest son Sir Peter became head of the family. Sir Peter Colleton was one of the eight proprietors of Carolina, a member of the Barbados Council, and owner of a large Barbados sugar plantation manned by 180 slaves. Sir Peter could afford the luxury of living in England, leaving the management of his Barbados property to his younger brother Thomas. Though overshadowed by Sir Peter, Thomas Colleton was a leading figure on the island also; he sat on the assembly, was a colonel of the militia, and a judge on the Barbados bench. A third brother, James Colleton, had no fruitful role in Barbados, and could rise to no office higher than vestryman for the local parish. So he came to Carolina, took out extensive land grants, and served as governor of the colony from 1686 to 1690. But the rambunctious Carolinians rose up in rebellion against James Colleton in 1690 and banished him from the colony. Poor James retreated back to Barbados. At this juncture, brother Thomas conveniently died or retired to England, which opened a slot at last for James in Barbados. In 1692 he assumed management of Colleton plantation, and soon took his brother's seat in the Barbados Assembly, doubtless delighted at having escaped so well from South Carolina.[8]

People like the Colletons and Middletons were drawn to Carolina because of its semi-tropical setting, which seemed to combine the advantages of Caribbean agriculture with the wholesome environment of the North American mainland. These island planters must have been convinced, after two generations of experience, that the West Indies were unhealthy for white men. The English islands in the West Indies had an appallingly high mortality rate in the late seventeenth century. Every index confirms this fact. For example, baptismal and burial registers for Barbados in 1678-1679 show that nearly twice as many whites were buried as were baptized on this island during an eighteen month period.[9] Vital statistics are very spotty for Barbados during the seventeenth century, but there is a broken series of baptismal and burial registers for the parish which embraces Bridgetown, the chief port, from 1648 onwards. These registers corroborate the evidence in the census of 1680 that Bridgetown was an exceptionally sickly community. In good years, three persons were buried for every one baptized; in bad years, five persons were buried for every one baptized.[10] Out in the Barbados countryside, the birth-death ratio seems to have been more evenly balanced. But the vital statistics we have for two rural parishes in Jamaica suggest that the white population in these districts became increasingly unhealthy as the century wore on. At first, in the 1660s and 1670s, births outnumbered deaths in both parishes, but after 1680 the burials always outnumbered the baptisms, generally by two to one.[11]

Another—and perhaps rather eccentric—method I have employed for judging the West Indian mortality rate is to examine the inscriptions on ancient tombstones, to see how old the colonists were when they

8 The vestry records for St. John's parish, Barbados (Barbados Museum Library, St. Ann's Garrison) show that all three Colleton brothers were annually elected to the vestry in the mid-1670's, until Sir Peter left for England. James continued to serve on the vestry until 1686, when he went to Carolina, and Thomas served until 1691. The next year, James was back on the vestry and served throughout the decade. James entered the Barbados Assembly in 1694 and sat until at least 1700 (*Journal of the Barbados Museum and Historical Society*, XI [1944], 171-173).

9 Dunn, "The Barbados Census of 1680," 24-25.

10 St. Michael's parish register, Barbados Archives, RL 1/1. My computation is based on totals for the following fourteen years: 1648-1650, 1657-1658, 1661-1662, 1670, 1674, 1678, 1682, 1686, 1690 and 1694.

11 St. Andrew, Register of Baptisms, Marriages, Burials, 1664-1750; St. Catherine, Register, 1669-1750, Island Registry Office, Spanish Town, Jamaica. In both the Jamaica and Barbados parish registers, I suspect that deaths were recorded more completely than births. But this would not explain the changing birth-death ratio in the two Jamaica parishes.

died. More than 350 Jamaica and Barbados tombstones for the years 1670-1750 record the person's age at death. Tomb-counting has obvious statistical defects. A grave marker in the West Indies was a status symbol at this time, and the people memorialized were mostly from the planter or merchant classes. The young and the old were inadequately represented, the young because their parents generally did not bother to set up stones for them, the old because they frequently retired to England. Nevertheless, for what it is worth, my sample shows that these island people died very young. White males who survived to age twenty, which was half the total number born at best, died at a median age of forty-five. Females who survived to age twenty died at a median age of thirty-six. The nine-year sex differential is grim testimony to the ravages of child-bearing in the tropics, but the overall sample shows low life expectancy for both sexes, with scarcely anyone lasting past age seventy.[12]

Because of this crippling death rate, Englishmen in the sugar islands found it difficult to establish a healthy family structure in the late seventeenth century. The Barbados and Jamaica parish registers are unfortunately too incomplete to permit the "family reconstitution" which European demographers practice. It is evident from these registers that West Indian couples could produce up to a dozen children, but that they often lost all of their offspring in infancy and childhood. The Barbados census of 1680 gives a devastating demographic profile of the population of Bridgetown at this date. Family life in this port town was severely stunted in 1680. One third of the householders were unmarried or widowed, the majority of householders were childless, and few married couples had more than one or two living children. I doubt, however, that traditional domestic patterns were ever so ruptured in the Barbados countryside. We have no solid evidence on this point, however, until 1715, when another census was taken which listed the age and sex of every white person on the island. According to this census, Barbados in 1715 had a very young white population; the median age was nineteen, and only three per cent of the inhabitants had passed their sixtieth birthday. But it was not a growing population, because only

12 My sample consists of 286 tombs of males and females aged 20 or over, recorded in Philip Wright, *Monumental Inscriptions of Jamaica* (London, 1966), and 46 tombs of males and females, aged 20 or over, recorded in E. M. Shilstone, *Monumental Inscriptions in the Burial Ground of the Jewish Synagogue at Bridgetown, Barbados* (n. p. [1956]). All of these tombs are pre-1750. A good many of the Barbados Jews lived past 70, but the majority died very young, and their median age at death is almost identical with the Jamaica Christians.

half the adults were married, and married couples had small families. There were many widows, widowers and orphans; also many mulattos, demonstrating widespread miscegenation. On the whole, conditions in Barbados do seem to have improved demographically between 1680 and 1715. The average Barbados family in 1715 had two living children, double the figure for Bridgetown in 1680. But this was still well below the norm for the mainland colonies at this date.[13] It would be interesting to see whether the Barbadians who migrated to South Carolina did in fact live longer, produce more children, and develop a healthier family structure than the colonists who stayed in the sugar islands.

The sugar planters naturally blamed the Caribbean environment for the debilitating diseases and early deaths they suffered. White men, so the argument ran, could not tolerate tropical heat, humidity and insect life. But the sugar planters might well have blamed themselves. Englishmen who settled in the West Indies during the seventeenth century were not very successful in accommodating themselves to an alien environment. They retained English habits ill-suited to the tropical climate and developed new habits ill-suited to any climate.

It is not altogether easy to reconstruct the lifestyle of the island colonists at the time South Carolina was founded. The sugar planters kept no diaries and left few personal papers. Fortunately, a number of visitors to the islands wrote graphic descriptions of what they saw. A few seventeenth-century houses and bits of furniture survive in Barbados and Jamaica, and the archaeological work now in progress at Port Royal, Jamaica is of capital importance; it will likely uncover a great slice of social data as of 1692 when an earthquake swamped this Jamaican town.

Another approach, which I have attempted, is to examine inventories of estates, compiled for probate purposes. Only scattered early inventories have survived in Barbados and the Leeward Islands. But there are some 800 Jamaican inventories in the Spanish Town archives, spanning the years from 1674 to 1701, which tell a lot about how the typical big planter, small planter, merchant, shopkeeper and artisan

13 Patricia Molen has analyzed this census in "Barbados, 1715—Population and Society" (unpublished seminar paper, The Johns Hopkins University, 1968). Miss Molen concentrated on St. Peter's parish, and her conclusions support my analysis of the Christ Church parish return for 1715, printed in *Journal of the Barbados Museum and Historical Society*, V, 194-203; VI, 41-44, 7-90, 152-159, 218-223; VII, 50-53, 87-93.

lived during these years.[14] Some of these inventoried Jamaican estates are valued at less than £10, others at more than £10,000. Collectively, they differ markedly from late seventeenth-century inventories I have seen or read about in Massachusetts, Pennsylvania and Maryland. In Jamaica, more rich merchants and planters are represented than in the mainland colonies, and they parade their wealth more gorgeously. The Jamaica inventories exhibit a wide contrast between the living habits of the richest and poorest members of the community. Some colonists had a great deal of money and displayed it ostentatiously. Others had none and lived in grinding poverty.[15]

For example, Samuel Long, one of the richest sugar planters in Jamaica, owned 11,000 acres and 288 slaves when he died at age 45. He had two expensively furnished houses, one at his chief plantation and the other at Port Royal. In this town house, the hall was sizable enough to hold sixty chairs and seven tables. In his dining room, Long had a dozen table cloths, twelve dozen napkins, and £76 worth of silver to dress his table. His wardrobe contained garments which cost more individually than the entire household furnishings of a typical small Jamaican farmer. At the opposite extreme, Ebenezer Hicks was a schoolmaster who owned a horse worth £2, furniture worth £1, and a parcel of books worth £1 when he died. He left no clothes, for he was buried in them. The parish owed him two years' back salary.

In most Jamaican inventories, large and small, Negro slaves were the chief asset. Five per cent of the people in the sample owned sixty or more slaves; these were the big sugar planters. But on the other hand, seventy per cent held at least one slave. Almost all the Jamaican farmers whose estates were inventoried, many of them very poor men, owned Negroes. The rich Jamaicans kept some Negroes for show rather than work, dressing them

14 Inventories, I B/11/Liber 1-3, 5, Jamaica Archives, Spanish Town. Liber 4 (1694-1699) is missing. The series continues into the eighteenth century. The following remarks are based on my examination of 600 of these inventories.

15 For purposes of comparison, I have examined 250 Massachusetts inventories, 1670-1700, from the Suffolk Co. Probate Court Records, vols. 5, 7-14 (microfilm 689: 2-5, University of Pennsylvania Library). For Pennsylvania inventories of this period, see Gary B. Nash, *Quakers and Politics* (Princeton, 1968), pp. 281-285. For Maryland inventories, see Aubrey C. Land, "Economic Base and Social Structure: The Northern Chesapeake in the Eighteenth Century," *Journal of Economic History*, XXV (1965), 641-646. Generally speaking, a Jamaican estate announced at £500 was worth about the same as a £500 estate in Maryland, and two or three times as much as a £500 estate in Massachusetts or Pennsylvania. This is because the Massachusetts and Pennsylvania appraisers included land and buildings, and because they valued property at a consistently higher rate.

up in livery and assigning them ceremonial tasks. A Port Royal clergyman complained in 1687 that "a cooper's wife shall go forth in the best flowered silk and richest silver and gold lace that England can afford, with a couple of Negroes at her tail."[16] Nearly ten per cent of these Jamaicans owned Indian slaves, used for hunting wild game and fishing. This helps explain why the Caribbean colonists, when they moved to Carolina, quickly developed an active Indian slave trade. South Carolina has the distinction of enslaving many more Indians than any other mainland colony.

The contrast between the eating habits of the upper and lower classes in the sugar islands was tremendous. The black slaves and white servants ate a monotonous and meager diet of corn, plantains, cassava bread, and—if they were lucky—salt fish and salt meat. They got drunk on rum every weekend. Members of the master class dined richly and drank copiously every day of the week. The main repast was mid-day dinner as in England, though this is a very hot time of day for heavy eating in the tropics. Dinner and after-dinner drinking lasted four or five hours if company was present. Roast meats, pies and custards, the diet of the upper class back home in England, dominated the planter's menu. In the cool of the evening at Port Royal, the merchants gathered at the taverns to eat cheese cake, tarts, creams, custards and sillabub, made as precisely as possible after the recipes of London pastry cooks. Nearly every planter kept a lusty bowl of cold rum punch ready on his table to accommodate friends and visitors, but since rum was considered a common and coarse drink, the island elite preferred to drink madeira and brandy.[17] Around 1700 a Barbados planter described the annual Cockney feast, celebrated by all the island gentry born within the sound of Bow Bell in London. The company breakfasted on plum broth, marched to church for a sermon, and repaired to an elaborately decorated hall where they were summoned to dinner by twelve trumpeters. Each course of the banquet was punctuated by a toast and a volley of twenty-five guns! The more tenacious members of the party were still toasting and firing guns at midnight.[18]

16 The Rev. Francis Crow to Giles Firmin, 7 March 1686/7, *Jamaican Historical Review*, III, 54.

17 Richard Ligon, *History of Barbados*, 27-39; John Taylor, "Present State of Jamaica," [1688], MSS. at Institute of Jamaica, Kingston, pp. 500-504, 536-540; Neville Connell. ed., "Father Labat's Visit to Barbados in 1700," *Journal of the Barbados Museum and Historical Society*, XXIV. 165, 172-173.

18 T. Walduck to James Petiver, 1710, *Journal of the Barbados Museum and Historical Society*, XV, 45-47.

In short, the sugar planters ate too much heavy food for their own good, their servants and slaves ate too little, and everyone drank too much.

In clothing style as in dietary habits, the English refused to accept tropical realities. The late seventeenth century was a period when extremely elaborate costume was fashionable at home, and island ladies with money spent it on wired headdresses, corsets, bustles, layers of petticoats, and luxuriously textured skirts which trailed the ground. The island gentlemen sported periwigs, full-skirted coats, embroidered waistcoats and sleeves, flowing cravats, and beribboned knee breeches. The Jamaica inventories show that the shops of Port Royal were amply stocked with cases of flowered silk, boxes of lace, white kid gloves, beaver hats, silk hose, laced pumps, and leather fans. The islanders favored clothing made of linen, silk or calico, but many of their suits and cloaks were made of wool. Little of this clothing was given to the slaves, who went almost naked. Male Negroes generally wore drawers, and females wore skirts. The white servants wore much the same costume as agricultural laborers at home, including Monmouth caps, which being brimless, cannot have provided much protection from the sun. The wealthy planters and their wives wished to keep their complexions as white as possible, in contrast to their black-skinned slaves and rednecked servants. Consequently, they wore hoods or broad-brimmed hats, neckcloths, stockings and gloves. With all this ostentatious overdressing, the island elite probably suffered more from the humid heat than did their servants and slaves.[19]

As with food and clothing, so with housing. Nearly all of the early buildings in the English islands have been obliterated by storms and fires, but we can tell from descriptions and inventories that the rich sugar planters built elaborate dwellings, sumptuously furnished. Visitors late in the century always described them as constructed "in the English style" or "after the English manner." This meant using brick or stone in preference to wood and plaster, building multi-storied houses in preference to wide, low bungalows, and using glazed windows rather than louvres or shutters. About 1695, Samuel Copen drew a panoramic "Prospect of Bridgetown in Barbados" which makes this Caribbean port look indistinguishable from a commercial town in England or Holland. The houses press close to the wharves, leaving no

19 Sir Hans Sloane, *A Voyage to the Islands Madera, Barbados, Nieves, S. Christophers and Jamaica*, I (London, 1707), xlvii, liv; J. C. Jeaffreson, *A Young Squire of the Seventeenth Century* (2 vols. London, 1878), I, 233-236, 248, 269-270.

room for gardens or shade trees. They are tall and narrow structures, three to five stories in height, without balconies or verandahs. This architectural style was better geared to Northern Europe than to the Caribbean. As Sir Hans Sloane observed when he visited Jamaica in 1687, the old Spanish houses on the island were designed for maximum coolness and to withstand tropical storms, whereas the new English houses "are neither cool, nor able to endure the shocks of Earthquakes." No wonder the English found it necessary to install great fans in their parlors and lounged half prostrate much of the time in hammocks. No wonder Sloane found that the planters liked to sit up half the night drinking, for when they went to bed they almost suffocated inside four-poster beds, enveloped by curtains, to keep out the bad night air. We learn from the inventory of his household goods that Sir Henry Morgan, the buccaneer king, slept in a silken nightgown on a costly bed equipped with mohair curtains, persian lining, and a "musketo nett." His servants, who slept in hammocks, and even his slaves, who slept on the ground, were very likely more comfortable.[20]

Perhaps the sugar planters insisted so strenuously on English styles and English standards because they felt imperiled by the volatile Caribbean atmosphere. Nothing seemed permanent in the West Indies. A hurricane or an epidemic disease or a slave revolt or a French invasion could wipe out the most flourishing plantation overnight. It was a boom-and-bust way of life. The whites felt swamped by their black slaves, yet enjoyed lording it over them. For all their *nouveau riche* pursuit of English genteel standards, the sugar planters lived like no Englishmen at home. Their milieu was hectic, frantic. They grew rich fast, spent recklessly, played desperately, and died young. At the time South Carolina was founded, they had made their beautiful islands almost uninhabitable. Those who moved to Carolina may have sought escape from this style of life, yet surely they carried much of it with them.

Most basically, the islanders introduced Negro slavery to South Carolina. The institution of chattel slavery would have developed in colonial Carolina in any case, but certainly the island immigrants gave it an early boost. Starting with Sir John Yeamans in 1671, members of the big sugar planting families brought gangs of Negroes with them to South Carolina. I suspect that many of the poor whites who came from the islands also brought a slave or two.

20 Samuel Copen, "A Prospect of Bridgetown in Barbados," copperplate engraving by J. Kip (London, 1695), Cunard Gallery, Barbados Museum; Sloane, *A Voyage to the Islands*, I, x, xlvii; inventory of Sir Henry Morgan's estate, 1 B/11/Liber 3, Jamaica Archives.

In the 1680s and 1690s, before the introduction of rice as a staple crop, the colony already had a sizable Negro labor force. Lowland Carolina would soon have a population ratio of four blacks to every white, not far different from the ratio in Barbados.

Carolina rice planters of the eighteenth century had more in common with Barbados sugar planters of the seventeenth century than large gangs of slaves. They too grew rich overnight. They too developed a proud and mettlesome school of politics. They too fashioned an aristocratic elite in which wealth, privilege and power were closely correlated. To be sure, the Carolinians adjusted more successfully to their semi-tropical environment than had Englishmen in the Caribbean. But Charles Town's brittle, gay and showy style of life echoed the Barbados milieu of a century before. Both societies displayed a remarkable compound of old world elegance and frontier boisterousness. In 1773 the *South Carolina Gazette* commented wryly on the aggressive habits of the Carolina gentry: "Their whole Lives are one continued Race: in which everyone is endeavoring to distance all behind him; and to overtake or pass by, all before him. ... Every Tradesman is a Merchant, every Merchant is a Gentleman, and every Gentleman one of the Noblesse. We are a Country of Gentry. ... We have no such thing as a common People among us: Between Vanity and Fashion the species is utterly destroyed."[21] One hundred years before, the Barbadoes gentry had been caught up in the same sort of continual race, sustained by vanity and fashion. And when some of them moved to Carolina, they kept on running. So it was that these Caribbean pioneers helped to create on the North American coast a slave-based plantation society closer in temper to the islands they fled from than to any other mainland English settlement.

21 Quoted by Carl Bridenbaugh, *Myths and Realities* (Baton Rouge, 1952), p. 115.

Colonial South Carolina and the Caribbean Connection

Jack P. Greene
Professor, Department of History
Johns Hopkins University

*Originally published in the
South Carolina Historical and Archaeological Magazine
Volume 88, Number 4 (October 1987)*

Within the leavings of the Hispanic and Portuguese American Empires during the first half of the seventeenth century, English adventurers established viable settlements in four separate areas: the Chesapeake, Bermuda, New England, and Barbados. Notwithstanding the fact that they all shared a common English heritage, no two of the new societies that emerged out of these settlements were alike, and three of them—those in the Chesapeake, New England, and Barbados—became what some cultural geographers refer to as culture hearths. That is, they became sites for the creation of powerful local cultures, including social institutions and ways of manipulating a particular kind of environment, that proved to be remarkably capable of recreation and, with appropriate modifications, transferable to other areas in the Anglo-American world.

Historians have long been familiar with the processes by which the tobacco and mixed farming culture of Virginia spread north into Maryland, Delaware, and parts of Pennsylvania and south into North Carolina and by which the mixed-farming and fishing culture of Puritan Massachusetts Bay extended itself into offshoot societies in Connecticut, Rhode Island, New Haven, New Hampshire, Long Island, New Jersey, and Maine. Until recently, they have paid far less attention to the equally fecund staple agricultural culture of Barbados. During the last half of the seventeenth century, the culture first articulated in Barbados slowly spread to the nearby Leeward Islands in the eastern Caribbean and, after its capture from the Spaniards in 1655, to the large island of Jamaica in the central Caribbean. After 1750, a variant strain of that culture, developed—within the English world, in the Leeward Island colonies of St. Kitts, Antigua, Nevis, and Montserrat—found a congenial setting in the new British West Indian island colonies of the Virgin Islands, Grenada, St. Vincent, Dominica, and Tobago.

As most South Carolinians familiar with their early history will know, however, the extension of Barbadian culture went beyond the West Indies to the North American mainland. Established in 1670 with some small settlements near the confluence of the Ashley and Cooper Rivers, South Carolina and the Lower South culture that developed out of those small beginnings and gradually spread north to the Cape Fear region of North Carolina and south into Georgia and East and West Florida, was as much the offspring of Barbados as was Jamaica or the other English Caribbean colonies.

Although scholars have long appreciated the role of Barbados in the origins of the Lower South, the sudden and artificial separation of the North American continental colonies from the West Indian colonies as a result of the American Revolution and the simultaneous incorporation of South Carolina and Georgia into the larger American culture of the United States have tended to focus attention away from the continuing vibrancy of South Carolina's Caribbean connection throughout the colonial period. The same developments have also tended to obscure the related fact that, for much of its colonial existence, South Carolina exhibited socio-economic and cultural patterns that, in many important respects, corresponded more closely to those in the Caribbean colonies than to those in the mainland colonies to the north. Though it is still far from complete, new work over the past fifteen years on the social history of Britain's early modern colonies now makes it more possible than ever before to analyze the developmental parallels and contrasts among the several colonies that trace their origins in some major part to the Barbados culture hearth.

II

This essay will explore three themes: first, South Carolina's Caribbean roots; second, its continuing connection with the Caribbean colonies during the colonial period; and third, the developmental parallels between it and the other colonies—the Leeward Islands and Jamaica—that emerged out of the Barbadian culture hearth during the seventeenth and early eighteenth centuries.

Why Barbados became a base and a prototype for the establishment of so many other colonies in the Caribbean and in the Lower South can only be explained by an examination of its early history. For ten years after its initial settlement in 1627, Barbados, like earlier English colonies in Virginia and Bermuda, concentrated very largely on tobacco culture, though it also began producing considerable quantities of cotton and indigo during the late 1630s. From the beginning, Barbados was a reasonably successful producer of staples for the English market, and this success drew large numbers of English immigrants to it and set off a feverish rush for land that, within a decade, had resulted in the occupation of virtually all of the arable land both in Barbados, which covered an area of only 166 square miles and in the nearby Leeward Islands, all four of which covered an area of only 251 square miles.[1]

As had been the case in early Virginia, the entire society was organized for profit. A few people from English gentry and commercial families, mostly younger sons, came to make their fortunes, but most immigrants were single male dependent indentured servants imported to labor in the cultivation and processing of tobacco, cotton, and indigo. Every bit as competitive, exploitative, and materialistic as early Virginia, Barbados experienced a rapid concentration of wealth, as the society polarized into small groups of proprietors and a mass of dependent indentured servants or mobile free laborers. Paying but scant attention to religion or other social and cultural institutions, Barbados and the Leeward Islands were notorious for their riotous and abandoned styles of life, while high mortality among new immigrants and the imbalance of women in the population contributed to the slow process of family development.[2]

Most of these early tendencies were even further enhanced by the gradual substitution of sugar for minor staple cultivation beginning in Barbados in the mid-1640s and gradually extending to the Leeward Islands and Jamaica in subsequent decades. This capital and labor intensive crop led to the further concentration of property into the hands of the few people who could command the capital to purchase the labor and equipment necessary to produce sugar competitively. At the same time they were amassing larger and larger estates for themselves, these plantation owners were replacing white servants and free white laborers with African slaves, who seem to have been both a more economical and a more reliable source of labor. Like their counterparts in Virginia, Barbadian planters had, from the beginning of settlement, shown no reluctance to treat white servant labor as a disposable commodity, and the wholesale importation of African slaves into Barbados and the Leeward Islands represented both a logical extension of that impulse and the first large-scale use of slavery and non-European labor in any of the English colonies.

1 F.C. Innes, "The Pre-Sugar Era of European Settlement in Barbados," *Journal of Caribbean History* I (1970): 1-22; Richard S. Dunn, *Sugar and Slaves: The Rise of the Planter Class in the English West Indies, 1624-1713* (Chapel Hill, 1972), pp. 46-59, and "Experiments Holy and Unholy, 1630-1," in K.R. Andrews, N.P. Canny, and P.E. Hair, eds., *The Westward Enterprise: English Activities in Ireland, the Atlantic, and America 1480-1650* (Detroit, 1979), pp. 272-75; Richard B. Sheridan, *Sugar and Slavery: Economic History of the British West Indies 1623-1775* (Baltimore, 1974), pp. 75-96, 123; Richard Pares, *Merchants and Planters* (Cambridge, 1960), pp. 1-25.

2 Dunn, *Sugar and Slaves*, pp. 263-334; Babette M. Levy, "Early Puritanism in the Southern and Island Colonies," *American Antiquarian Society Proceedings* LXX (1961): 278-307.

By the early 1650s, as a result of the sugar revolution, Barbados had achieved a population density greater than any comparable area in the English-speaking world, except London. But the introduction of black slaves into Barbados contributed to a rapid decline of white population, as many whites migrated to other colonies where there were greater opportunities to acquire land or returned to England. From a high of about 30,000 in 1650, the number of whites fell to about 20,000 in 1680 and 15,500 in 1700. Despite the fall in numbers of white settlers, Barbados, in 1670, was certainly, as Richard S. Dunn has written, "the richest, most highly developed, most populous, and most congested English colony in America, with a thriving sugar industry and 50,000 inhabitants, including 30,000 Negroes."

As Barbados and its neighboring colonies in the Leeward Islands became more black and the concentration on sugar production became ever more intensive, profits soared and wealth accumulation among the possessing classes was phenomenal. By 1660, the wealth of Barbados, the earliest and best developed of the island colonies, exceeded that of any other contemporary English overseas possession. But the rapid rise of a wealthy and conspicuous elite did not immediately give either much cohesion or stability to Barbadian society. Indeed, many of those wealthy few proprietors who could afford it began to flee the tropical sugar factories they had established for the more settled and, especially after 1680, healthier world of England.[3]

That the socio-economic model first successfully articulated in Barbados with its exploitative and materialistic orientation, concentration on sugar production, a slave-powered plantation system, a highly stratified social structure, great disparities in wealth and styles of life, a high ratio of blacks to whites, little attention to the development of family life and other traditional social institutions and cultural amenities, high levels of absenteeism among the wealthy, a rapid turnover among the elite, and heavy mortality—that Barbadian cultural system also came to characterize the four neighboring Leeward Island colonies is scarcely surprising. In part because of the concentration of capital and labor in Barbados and

3 Carl and Roberta Bridenbaugh, *No Peace Beyond the Line: The English in the Caribbean, 1624-690* (New York, 1972), pp. 165-305 ; Dunn, *Sugar and Slaves*, pp. 59- 83, 117-26, 188-264, "Experiments Holy and Unholy," pp. 285-89, and "The English Sugar Islands and the Founding of South Carolina," this *Magazine* LXXII (1971): 82; Sheridan, *Sugar and Slavery*, pp. 128-40; Hilary McD. Beckles, "Rebels and Reactionaries: The Political Response of White Labourers to Planter-Class Hegemony in Seventeenth-Century Barbados," *Journal of Caribbean History* XV (1981): 1-19, and "The Economic Origins of Black Slavery in the British West Indies, 1640-1680: A Tentative Analysis of the Barbados Model," *Journal of Caribbean History* XVI (1982): 36-56; John J. McCusker and Russell R. Menard, *The Economy of British America 1607-1789* (Chapel Hill, 1985), pp. 151-53.

in part because rivalries with the Dutch and French prevented English settlers from securing uncontested control over most of them until 1713, however, the Leeward Island colonies developed far more slowly than did Barbados and never attracted such a large white immigration. By the 1720s and 1730s, however, they had successfully emulated the experience of Barbados in the previous century.[4]

But the Barbadian model also proved capable of transfer beyond the Lesser Antilles in the eastern Caribbean to much larger physical entities in Jamaica and South Carolina. Settled by the English in the second half of the seventeenth century, these two colonies, like the Leeward Islands, also developed far more slowly than Barbados. But they eventually became highly successful plantation colonies on the Barbadian model. Indeed, by the mid-eighteenth century, they had become two of the three wealthiest and economically most important British-American colonies, with only Virginia—and not even Barbados—approaching them in this regard.

Continuously occupied by Spaniards since the early sixteenth century, Jamaica, prior to the English conquest in 1655, had been primarily a producer of livestock and minor staples, especially cocoa, and had never been an important part of the Hispanic American empire. With 4,411 square miles of territory, more than twenty-six and a half times that of Barbados and approximately the same size as the area that would later comprise the South Carolina lowcountry, Jamaica was first settled by disbanded English soldiers and the flow of excess population from England's eastern Caribbean colonies. This flow included many planters who, having made considerable fortunes in Barbados or the Leeward Islands migrated with their slaves to Jamaica, where they hoped to establish a new, and infinitely more expandable, sugar colony that would have land enough to enable them to provide for their younger sons. This migration began in earnest in 1664 when one of Jamaica's first governors, Sir Thomas Modyford, and some 700 other Barbadian planters arrived in the colony with their slaves.

Jamaica soon rivaled Barbados in riches. But in the early decades, its wealth came more from the activities of its freebooting buccaneers, who used its strategic position in the central Caribbean to tap the vast wealth of the Hispanic American empire. Through a combination of trade and raids, they converted their Jamaica base at Port Royal into the richest spot in English America. Primarily because it did not for many decades have access to a plentiful slave supply, however, Jamaica was slow to develop as a sugar-producing staple colony. Following the example of

4 Sheridan, *Sugar and Slavery*, pp. 148-207.

the Spaniards, all of whom had fled the colony within three or four years after the English conquest, leaving their large stocks of cattle behind, many of Jamaica's new proprietors raised cattle and other livestock for food consumption in Jamaica and elsewhere in the Caribbean, while others produced minor staples, including cocoa, indigo, and provisions. Not until the beginning of the eighteenth century did Jamaica export as much sugar as tiny Barbados.[5]

No less than the Leeward Islands and Jamaica, South Carolina also represented a successful extension of the Barbados culture hearth. As more and more of its arable land was converted to sugar and foodstuffs and other supplies had to be imported from elsewhere, Barbadian leaders began to look to the unoccupied portions of the southeastern mainland of North America as a potential site for new settlements that would be able to supply the provisions and other necessities required to sustain the island's sugar economy. With approval of the Lords Proprietors to whom, following his Restoration to the English throne in 1660, Charles II had granted authority to colonize Carolina and the Bahamas, a group of Barbadians, including the same Sir Thomas Modyford who settled in Jamaica in 1664, had unsuccessfully sought to establish settlements at Cape Fear and Port Royal in the mid-1660s.

As several historians have recently emphasized, Barbadians also played an extensive role in the first successful settlement in 1670. Almost half of the whites and considerably more than half of the blacks who came to the new settlement during the first two years were from Barbados, and this distribution continued for at least two decades. The most thorough and authoritative study we have of the origins of the 1,343 white settlers who immigrated to South Carolina between 1670 and 1690 indicates that more than 54 percent were probably from Barbados. They included people from all social classes. The great majority were from the small planter and freeman classes of families, a small planter owning at least ten acres but fewer than twenty slaves and a freeman owning less than ten acres. Some of these simply sold out and used the proceeds to transport themselves and their families and slaves to Carolina, while others came as indentured servants.

5 Dunn, *Sugar and Slaves*, pp. 149-87; Sheridan, *Sugar and Slavery*, pp. 92-96, 208-16; Orlando Patterson, *The Sociology of Slavery: An Analysis of the Origins, Development and Structure of Negro Slave Society in Jamaica* (Rutherford, N.J., 1969), pp. 15-69.

But South Carolina's Barbadian immigrants also included a few members of the island's elite. According to Dunn, representatives of eighteen of those 175 big Barbadian sugar planting families, which had at least sixty slaves apiece, "held the best land, sold the most sugar, and monopolized the chief offices on the island," obtained land in South Carolina. Not all of these families actually settled in the colony. But a significant number, including, among the earlier immigrants, Edward and Arthur Middleton, James Colleton, and Robert and Thomas Gibbes, did. Further research by Richard Waterhouse has shown that, in addition, "representatives of as many as thirty-three 'middling' [Barbadian] planter families settled in Carolina between 1670 and 1690," middling planters being those who owned between twenty and fifty-nine slaves. Finally, a number of Barbadian merchants acquired land in South Carolina. Although many of them used agents to manage their plantations, several, including John Ladson, Benjamin Quelch, and Bernard Schenckingh actually moved to the colony.

Not only did these Barbadians bring "energy, experience, and wealth" to South Carolina. They also brought the social and cultural system that had been so fully articulated in the island over the previous four decades. The only mainland English colony that began its existence with a preference for African slave labor and a significant number of African slaves among its original settlers, South Carolina early revealed that strong commercial, materialistic, and exploitative mentality that had found such a ready field for action in the Caribbean. For at least a generation, the colony functioned effectively as its West Indian proponents had initially intended, as an adjunct to the Barbadian economy. South Carolina developed a vigorous grazing economy that in size rivaled that of Jamaica, and, in return for sugar products and black slaves, it sent large quantities of beef, pork, corn, lumber, naval stores, and Indian slaves to Barbados, the Leeward Islands, and Jamaica.

Even in its earliest days, however, the South Carolina economy was never wholly dependent on trade to the Caribbean. Provisioning privateers and pirates and, even more important, trading with the large number of Indians residing in the southeastern part of the North American continent for great quantities of deerskins for export to England were also lucrative activities. No less than early Barbadians, however, early South Carolinians were avid in their search for a profitable agricultural staple that would do for their colony what sugar had done for Barbados. Early experiments with tobacco and indigo were reasonably successful, but it was not until the successful experimentation with rice in the 1690s that the colony's planters found a staple that was sufficiently profitable to provide the basis for a viable plantation system on the Barbadian model. Over the next three decades, rice, naval stores, provisions, and deerskins brought in the capital necessary to acquire the almost wholly African slave labor force that helped to give South Carolina such a close resemblance to its West Indian progenitors. Already by 1710 there were more blacks than whites in South Carolina. By 1720, blacks outnumbered whites by almost two to one, a far higher ratio than would ever be exhibited by any other English mainland colony.[6]

III

If, especially in recent decades, historians have tended to emphasize the extent to which, "more than any mainland colony," South Carolina's "roots and early commercial ties stretched toward Barbados and other islands of the English Caribbean," they have paid far less attention to the continuing vitality of that connection. Within the early modern British Empire, such connections were maintained through flows of people, goods, and ideas along the major arteries of trade. Of these various flows, that of people probably dropped to quite low levels during the eighteenth century. A small number of wealthy planters and merchants fled the island colonies throughout the eighteenth century. Though most of them went to Britain or to one of the more northerly colonies, especially Rhode Island and New York, a few came to South Carolina. The families of Rawlins Lowndes, which came from St. Kitts in 1730, and Eliza Lucas Pinckney, which came from Antigua in 1738, are conspicuous examples.[7]

But the fact was that few of the island colonies had an exportable population in the eighteenth century. Neither the Leeward Island colonies nor Jamaica ever seem to have had more than a few whites to

6 South Carolina's early development, including its relations with Barbados and the Leeward Islands, may be followed in John P. Thomas, Jr., "The Barbadians in Early South Carolina," this *Magazine* XXXI (193 0): 75-92; M. Eugene Sirmans, *Colonial South Carolina, 1663-1763* (Chapel Hill, 1966), pp. 1-100; Dunn, "English Sugar Islands and the Founding of South Carolina," pp. 81-93; Richard Waterhouse, "England, the Caribbean, and the Settlement of Carolina," *Journal of American Studies* IX (1975): 259-81; Converse D. Clowse, *Economic Beginnings in Colonial South Carolina* (Columbia, 1971); Peter H. Wood, *Black Majority: Negroes in Colonial South Carolina from 1670 through the Stono Rebellion* (New York, 1974), pp. 3-194; Clarence L. Ver Steeg, *Origins of a Southern Mosaic: Studies of Early Carolina and Georgia* (Athens, 1975), pp. 103-32; Philip M. Brown, "Early Indian Trade in the Development of South Carolina: Politics, Economics, and Social Mobility during the Proprietary Period, 1670-1719," this *Magazine* LXXVI (1975): 118-28.

7 Wood, *Black Majority*, p. 55; Elise Pinckney, *The Letterbook of Eliza Lucas Pinckney 1739-1762* (Chapel Hill, 1972), pp. xv-xxvi.

spare, while Barbados experienced a reversal in its long-term decline of white population after 1710. Perhaps the result of improving health conditions, the number of whites in Barbados rose by almost 50 percent from a low of 13,000 in 1710 to around 18,500 in 1773. Although it had a rising, rather than a falling, white population, Barbados probably sent few of its whites to other colonies after 1710. With regard to the black population, all of the West Indian colonies, including Barbados, experienced high slave mortality of from 2 percent to 6 percent annually throughout the eighteenth century and had to maintain imports at that level just to keep the slave population from declining in absolute numbers.[8]

Although the stream of immigrants from the West Indies to South Carolina all but dried up in the eighteenth century, the flow of goods remained strong. In addition to small quantities of wine, limes, lime juice, cocoa, coffee, and sugar, South Carolina imported directly from the West Indies between 70 percent and 85 percent of the roughly 1,000 hogsheads each of sugar and molasses and 4,000 hogsheads of rum it consumed each year. Down through the 1730s, Barbados was the primary source of these sugar products, but both the Leeward Islands and Jamaica surpassed Barbados in the 1750s and 1760s.

In return, South Carolina shipped a variety of products to all of the West Indian colonies. Exports of naval stores were high early in the century but diminished over time; beef and pork, corn and peas, and leather remained fairly steady over the whole period, with Jamaica, Barbados, and the Leeward Islands continuing to be the leading importers of each down into the 1760s. Exports of lumber, barrel staves, and shingles increased dramatically after 1750, with Jamaica usually taking the largest quantities followed by Barbados, Antigua, and St. Kitts. To the West Indies, as to Europe, South Carolina's leading export was rice. The island colonies took about 10 percent of South Carolina's total rice exports in 1717-20 and around 20 percent in the 1760s. Barbados was the largest market through the 1730s, but it had fallen to third place behind Jamaica and the Leeward Islands by the late 1750s.

Altogether, in most years during the eighteenth century, about a fourth to a third of the total tonnage entering Charleston came from or via the West Indies, while between 15 percent to 25 percent of the ships cleared from Charleston traded to the West Indies. This disparity can

8 McCusker and Menard, *Economy of British America*, pp. 153-54; Sheridan, *Sugar and Slavery*, pp. 123, 502-6; Robert V. Wells, *The Population of the British Colonies in America before 1776: A Survey of Census Data* (Princeton, 1975), pp. 194-251.

be partly explained by contemporary shipping routes. Prevailing wind patterns dictated that many vessels from Britain came via the West Indies, while return voyages usually proceeded directly back to Britain. Although more ships entered Charleston from the West Indies than returned, by the 1760s, nearly forty ships based in the West Indies annually cleared the port of Charleston with return cargoes of rice and other commodities for Jamaica, Barbados, the Leeward Islands, and the Bahamas.[9]

This steady flow of goods back and forth between South Carolina and the West Indies brought news, ideas, even architectural innovations. The published business correspondence of Robert Pringle and Henry Laurens contain frequent correspondence with trading partners in Bridgetown, Barbados, and elsewhere in the West Indies, and the *South Carolina Gazette* often reprinted items from island newspapers, and vice versa. Especially interesting to South Carolina readers was news of the frequent slave uprisings in Jamaica and other sugar islands. As a recent architectural historian has shown, the verandah or front porch, first developed in the West Indies, appeared almost simultaneously about 1735 in most of the North American colonies engaged in the West Indian trade, including South Carolina.

IV

For South Carolina, these continuing connections were made more palpable by the obvious similarities between its own social development and that of the major West Indian colonies of Barbados, the Leeward Islands, and Jamaica. During the eighteenth century, however, no two of these products of the Barbados culture hearth followed precisely the same culture.

As declining soil fertility and higher processing costs required more and more capital and labor to yield ever-diminishing rates of return, Barbados continued its inexorable movement toward "a capital-intensive, power-intensive system of agriculture conducted on a sustain-yield basis." But the drive toward intensive sugar monoculture and many of the tendencies associated with that drive either lost vigor or changed in character between 1700 and 1775. By the 1730s, Barbados exhibited an actual turning away from sugar to livestock, and the movement towards property consolidation had leveled off by 1750, with roughly a third of the proprietors owning somewhat more than half of the estates and

9 The figures are derived from Converse D. Clowse, *Measuring Charleston's Overseas Commerce, 1717-1767: Statistics from the Port's Naval Lists* (Washington, D.C., 1981).

sugar mills. By mid-century, the colony, once again exhibiting a spirit of innovation of the kind it had demonstrated a century earlier during the sugar revolution, was responding to its increasingly unfavorable place in the Atlantic sugar market by successfully developing methods to produce more sugar byproducts, methods that yielded almost 50 percent more rum than the British West Indian average.

Despite these innovations, neither the size of estates nor the rate of profit was high enough to support much absenteeism among the large planter families, who exhibited a persistence and a commitment to the colony that defied the stereotype of early modern West Indian planter society. Nor were more than 20 percent to 25 percent of the island's whites members of the large estate owning class. About a quarter belonged to an intermediate class of officeholders, small merchants, professionals, estate managers, and small estate owners who produced cotton and foodstuffs on less than 100 acres. The rest consisted of a numerous class of poor whites, families with ten acres or less who lived largely on the margins of the plantation system, many in considerable poverty. After 1710, all classes of whites in Barbados enjoyed more favorable health conditions than did settlers elsewhere in the Caribbean, on the southern North American mainland, or even in continental cities such as Boston and Philadelphia.

Along with the steady growth in white population between 1710 and 1775, the slave population continued to rise, increasing by nearly three-fourths over the same period to over 68,500. Slave imports remained fairly high, but they accounted for a declining proportion of the slave population. With falling profits, planters found it more economical to provide better diet and health care in an effort to breed slaves locally and so save the costs of high annual replacements. Better living conditions and a growing ratio of seasoned creoles to the total number of slaves combined to lower annual mortality rates among Barbadian slaves from about 6 percent during the first quarter of the century to 3.8 percent during the third quarter. The ratio of blacks to whites levelled off at around four to one between 1750 and 1780.[10]

10 Sheridan, *Sugar and Slavery,* pp. 124-47; McCusker and Menard, *Economy of British America,* pp. 165-66; Karl Watson, *The Civilised Island Barbados: A Social History 1750-1816* (Bridgetown, 1979), pp. 30-125; Wells, *Population of the British Colonies,* pp. 236-51; Gary A. Puckrein, *Little England: Plantation Society and AngloBarbadian Politics, 1627-1700* (New York, 1984), pp. 181-94; Hilary Beckles, *Black Rebellion in Barbados: The Struggle Against Slavery, 1627-1838* (Bridgetown, 1984), pp. 52-85.

By contrast, the Leeward Islands showed no tendency to turn away from the drive toward sugar monoculture and no reversal in the decline of white settlers. In Nevis and Montserrat, the smallest of those islands, there was a steady loss of whites from the 1670s to a low point in 1745, followed by a slight rise over the next decade and a continuing downward trend thereafter. In St. Kitts and Antigua, which developed later, white population continued to climb into the 1720s and then dropped slowly thereafter.

Because the black populations tripled in all four islands between 1710 and 1780 and a substantial number of proprietors were absentees, perhaps as many as half in St. Kitts, the ratio of blacks to whites was much higher than in Barbados—15 to 1 in Antigua, 12 to 1 in St. Kitts, 11 to 1 in Nevis, and 7.5 to 1 in Montserrat. The result was that all four of the Leeward Islands were little more than a congeries of sugar factories with large concentrations of black slaves and quite small white populations that consisted of little more than a handful of white settler families, a few plantation managers, and a small intermediate class of merchants, lawyers, and doctors. The Leeward Islands thus represented an extreme version of the Barbadian model that perhaps more closely resembled a nineteenth-century industrial enterprise than the settler societies developing elsewhere in British America. Far more than Barbados, they were being transformed by the 1770s from colonies of settlement to colonies of exploitation with the impoverished cultural and political life usually associated with colonies of that category. The new colonies begun by the British in the West Indies after 1750 all tended to follow the Leeward Island example.[11]

Despite many similarities, Jamaica diverged considerably from the patterns exhibited by the smaller islands. Its sugar industry continued to grow slowly during the first four decades of the eighteenth century because of a variety of factors, including the secular decline of the British sugar market, the engrossment of some of the best sugar lands by large landholders who did not have the labor to exploit them, an inadequate slave supply, and the fierce opposition of the Maroons, bands of runaway slaves who lived in the inaccessible interior and terrorized outlying areas of the colony, especially between 1725 and 1739.

After the cessation of hostilities with the Maroons in 1739 and in response to a rising sugar market, Jamaica experienced spectacular

11 Sheridan, *Sugar and Slavery*, pp. 148-207; Wells, *Population of the British Colonies*. pp. 207-36: Margaret Deane Rouse-Jones, "St. Kitts, 1713-1763: A Study of the Development of a Plantation Society" (Ph.D. Diss., Johns Hopkins University, 1977).

economic growth from 1740 to 1775. The number of slaves and sugar estates doubled. By 1775, Jamaica was exporting ten times as many sugar products as Barbados and had three times as many slaves. Over the same period, the aggregate value of the colony's economy increased almost five times, from just over £3.5 million to over £15.1 million. It was far and away Britain's most valuable American colony. Its net worth per free white person was an astonishing £1,200 in 1775, more than nine times that found in the richest continental colonies in the upper and lower South.

But this rapid expansion produced significantly different results from those arising from the similar development of Barbados a century earlier or of the Leeward Islands a half century before. Jamaica never approached becoming a sugar monoculture. Four out of ten slaves were in nonsugar production, and more than half of the plantations were devoted to livestock, provisions, and minor staples. Also, slave mortality was considerably lower than in the Leeward Islands, ranging from 4 percent down to 2 percent annually, the probable result of better dietary standards deriving from the local custom of allowing each slave a small plot of provision ground and one and one-half days per week for his or her own activities. From the produce grown on these provision grounds, Jamaican slaves developed a vigorous internal marketing system. The growing size of the free black and colored population, which exceeded that of Barbados by ten to one, suggests that the slave system in the island, though it was both harsh and given to frequent revolts, was more easily escaped than elsewhere in the British Caribbean. Finally, there was much uncultivated land and considerable land wastage in Jamaica, where the plantation economy was more land-intensive and less labor- and capital-intensive.

Nor did Jamaica experience a loss of white population. Notwithstanding the facts that as high as 30 percent of the sugar plantation may have belonged to absentees by the mid-eighteenth century and that the ratio of blacks to whites climbed steadily from about 6.5 to 1 in 1703 to slightly more than 11 to 1 in 1775, white population increased slowly but steadily from 7,000 in 1703 to 18,000 in 1774. In contrast to that of the Leeward Islands, this population was not limited to a handful of resident managers of large sugar estates and a few professionals and local factors of London merchants. As in Barbados, as many as a fifth of island whites were from large landholding or wealthy and substantial mercantile or professional families, and there were many small planters, estate managers, urban artisans, clerks, and shopkeepers, many of whom lived in Kingston or Spanish Town, respectively Jamaica's chief port and capital. In the mid-1770s, Kingston, by far the largest urban place in the British West Indies, numbered over 11,000 inhabitants, including 5,000 whites, 1,200 free blacks and mulattoes, and 5,000 slaves.

Unlike the Leeward Islands but like Barbados, Jamaica managed, despite some absenteeism, to sustain a "self-conscious, articulate, cohesive social class of proprietor-administrators" well into the later eighteenth century. Like the large estate owners in Barbados, there were "committed settlers" who, especially after 1750, constructed grand houses in an emergent Jamaican vernacular style; supported an active press; built churches, schools, and hospitals; and exerted political and social control through dynamic and self-conscious local political institutions.[12]

In many ways, South Carolina's eighteenth-century development paralleled that of Jamaica. Its economic welfare was also closely tied to the fortunes of an external market for its principal staple. What sugar was for the West Indian colonies, rice became for South Carolina. Following its emergence in the 1690s, rice production as measured by exports grew steadily during the first three decades of the eighteenth century from 1.5 million pounds in 1710 to nearly 20 million by 1730. By the 1720s, it had become South Carolina's most valuable export, a position it held throughout the colonial period. Between 1730 and 1750, the rice market was erratic, and exports increased slowly, except for a brief period in the late 1730s. But starting in the early 1750s exports once again began to surge steadily upward. In terms of total value, rice, by the early 1770s, ranked fourth among exports from Britain's American colonies behind sugar, tobacco, and wheat.[13]

Like Jamaica, South Carolina never became monocultural, however. Throughout the colonial period, it continued to export most of its earliest products: deerskins, naval stores, lumber and barrel staves, grains, and meat. Beginning in the 1740s, the reintroduction of indigo by Eliza Lucas Pinckney and others and its successful production provided South Carolina with a second highly profitable staple, albeit one whose quality was not sufficiently high to sustain it following the withdrawal

12 Sheridan, *Sugar and Slavery*, pp. 208-33; McCusker and Menard, *Economy* of *British America*, p. 61; Wells, *Population* of *the British Colonies*, pp. 194-207; Edward Brathwaite, *The Development* of *Creole Society in Jamaica 1770-1820* (Oxford, 1971), pp. xiv, 8-175; Edward Long, *The History* of *Jamaica* (3 vols., London, 1774), II, p. 103.

13 McCusker and Menard, *Economy* of *British America*, pp. 175-80, 186-87; Daniel C. Littlefield, *Rice and Slaves: Ethnicity and the Slave Trade in Colonial South Carolina* (Baton Rouge, 1981), pp. 74-114; James M. Clifton, "The Rice Industry in Colonial America," *Agricultural History* LV (1981): 266-83; Henry C. Dethloff, "The Colonial Rice Trade," *Agricultural History* LVI (1982): 231-43; Peter A. Coclanis, "Rice Prices in the 1720s and the Evolution of the South Carolina Economy," *Journal* of *Southern History* XLVIII (1982): 531-44.

of a British bounty after the American Revolution. Around 1770, rice accounted for about 55 percent of the value of all exports, indigo for 20 percent, deerskins, naval stores and lumber products each for between 5 percent and 7 percent, and grain and meat products each for about 2 percent. The diversity of the South Carolina economy is illustrated by Robert M. Weir's calculation that the record rice crop of 1770 was grown by less than 50% of the slave population on no more than 3 percent of the land in private hands, while the largest harvest of indigo was grown by only about 13% of the slaves on less than 0.5 percent of such land.[14]

Also like Jamaica, staple agriculture brought South Carolina masses of black slaves, a precarious racial balance in the population, and enormous wealth. The black population rose dramatically from about 2,500 in 1700 to 5,000 in 1710, 39,000 in 1730, and 75,000 in 1770. Before 1720, South Carolina's black population seems to have been able to generate a natural increase. But with the intensification of staple agriculture in the 1720s and 1730s and, probably much more important, the importation of large numbers of new slaves from Africa, it began, like its counterparts in the West Indian colonies, to experience a net annual decrease. Though the slave population seems to have again become self-sustaining after 1750, most of the enormous increase in slaves was, throughout the colonial period, the result of large imports, which, except for the decade of the 1740s, remained high.[15]

Though it was greater by far than any other contemporary British continental colony, the ratio of blacks to whites for South Carolina as a whole never approached that in the Caribbean colonies. For most of the period after 1720, it seems to have remained roughly at 2 to 2.5 to 1. But these figures are deceptive. In some lowcountry parishes, the importation of blacks and the emigration of whites had, by the 1750s, raised the ratio as high as nine to one, a figure well beyond that found in Barbados and only slightly below that found in Jamaica. Such a racial distribution indeed made those parts of the lowcountry seem, in the words of one

14 G. Terry Sharrer, "The Indigo Bonanza in South Carolina, 1740-1790," *Technology and Culture* XII (1971): 447-55, and "Indigo in Carolina, 1671-1796," this *Magazine* LXXII (1971): 94-103 ; David L. Coon, "Eliza Pinckney and the Reintroduction of Indigo Culture in South Carolina," this *Magazine* LXXX (1979): 61-76; McCusker and Menard, *Economy of British America,* p. 174; Robert M. Weir, *Colonial South Carolina: A History* (Millwood, N.Y., 1983), p. 172.

15 Wood, *Black Majority,* pp. 131-66; "Estimated Population of the American Colonies: 1610-1780," in Jack P. Greene, ed., *Settlements to Society, 1584-1763: A Documentary History of the American Colonies* (New York, 1966), pp. 238-39.

contemporary, "more like a Negro country" than a settlement of people of European descent.[16]

Because of the proximity of the Spanish in Florida, the French in Louisiana, and many powerful Indian tribes, South Carolina, like the Caribbean colonies, already lived in persistent danger of external attack, and the large disproportion of blacks in the rural rice-growing areas gave the colony, again like those in the Caribbean, a potentially powerful domestic enemy. Based on that of Barbados, South Carolina's slave code was the most draconian on the continent, though some of the harshness that characterized Jamaican slavery may have been mitigated in South Carolina by the task system. Most South Carolina slaves worked not in gangs, like the sugar slaves of the Caribbean or the tobacco slaves of the Chesapeake, but by tasks, an arrangement that permitted the more industrious to grow their own produce and raise their own animals for sale to whites in a domestic marketing system that in its extent and economic importance probably approached that of Jamaica. For whatever reasons, South Carolina, in contrast to seventeenth-century Barbados and to Jamaica throughout the colonial period, both of which were riven by slave revolts, had only one major slave uprising, the Stono Rebellion of 1739. But the specter of slave revolt always lurked in the background. Also like the situation in the Caribbean colonies, South Carolina seems to have had a higher incidence of interracial sexual unions than any other colony on the continent.[17]

If staple agriculture and slavery brought South Carolina danger for whites and degradation for blacks, it also, by the middle of the eighteenth century, brought whites wealth that, while considerably less than that enjoyed by their counterparts in Jamaica, far exceeded that of any other settler population in British North America. Per capita wealth in the Charleston District of South Carolina in 1774 was an astonishing £2,337.7, more than four times that of people living in the tobacco areas of the Chesapeake and nearly six times greater than that of people living in the towns of New York and Philadelphia.

16 Wood, *Black Majority*, pp. 131-66.

17 M. Eugene Sirmans, "The Legal Status of the Slave in South Carolina, 1670-1740," *Journal of Southern History* XXVIII (1962): 462-73; Philip D. Morgan, "Work and Culture : The Task System and the World of Lowcountry Blacks, 1700 to 1880," *William & Mary Quarterly*, 3d ser., XXXIX (1982): 563-99; Michael Craton, *Testing the Chains: Resistance to Slavery in the British West Indies* (Ithaca, 1982), pp. 67-96, 105-79; David Barry Gaspar, *Bondmen and Rebels: A Study of Master-Slave Relations in Antigua with Implications of Colonial British America* (Baltimore, 1985); Beckles, *Black Rebellion in Barbados*, pp. 25-51; Wood, *Black Majority*, pp. 308-26; Winthrop D. Jordan, "American Chiaroscuro: The Status and Definition of Mulattoes in the British Colonies," *William & Mary Quarterly*, 3d ser., XIX (1962): 183-200.

This wealth enabled South Carolina's richest planters and merchants to live a luxurious life comparable to that of similar groups in seventeenth-century Barbados and eighteenth-century Jamaica. Beginning in the 1740s, members of this group built, usually in the English style but sometimes with some West Indian modifications, several expensive public buildings and many sumptuous private houses. Most wealthy rice planters chose Charleston as the site for their most elegant residence, and, with this large absentee planter class resident for much of the year, Charleston, a city of 11,000 by the 1770s, was a lively cultural center with a library company, concerts, theatre, horse races, and a variety of benevolent organizations, fraternal groups, and social clubs. By the 1770s, some South Carolina families had become sufficiently wealthy that they were even following the example of the West Indians and abandoning the colony altogether. In the early 1770s, as many as fifty absentee South Carolina proprietors were living in London.[18]

An important reason why England appealed to both West Indians and South Carolinians was the appalling health conditions that obtained in their home colonies. Life expectancy in South Carolina seems to have been slightly better than that in either Jamaica or the Leeward Islands, both of which were notorious for their high mortality among both whites and blacks. But both Charleston and lowcountry South Carolina suffered from a disease environment that was far more malignant than that of any other British continental colony. Crude death rates recently calculated for Charleston in the 1720s show that they were almost twice as high as those in contemporary Philadelphia or England and Wales.[19]

18 Alice Hanson Jones, *Wealth of a Nation To Be: The American Colonies on the Eve of the Revolution* (New York, 1980), p. 357; Richard Waterhouse, "The Development of Elite Culture in the Colonial American South: A Study of Charles Town, 1670-1770," *Australian Journal of Politics and History* XXVIII (1982): 391-404; Lewis P. Frisch, "The Fraternal and Charitable Societies of Colonial South Carolina" (B.A. Thesis, Johns Hopkins University, 1969); Diane Sydenham, " 'Going Home': South Carolinians in England, 1745-1775" (unpublished seminar paper, Johns Hopkins University, 1975).

19 Peter A. Coclanis, "Death in Early Charleston: An Estimate of the Crude Death Rate for the White Population of Charleston, 1722-1732," this *Magazine* LXXXV (1984): 280-91; H. Roy Merrens and George D. Terry, "Dying in Paradise: Malaria, Mortality, and the Perceptual Environment in Colonial South Carolina," *Journal of Southern History* L (1984): 533-50.

V

South Carolina had begun in the late seventeenth century as an offshoot of the prolific Barbadian culture hearth; although it lagged somewhat behind, in its subsequent demographic, socio-economic, and cultural development it thus closely paralleled that of Jamaica, Barbados's other principal seventeenth-century colony. Both South Carolina and Jamaica were heavily involved in the production of agricultural staples and both imported extraordinarily high numbers of African slaves that resulted in a population in which the numerical preponderance of blacks was overwhelming. As a result, both had a harsh system of labor discipline and lived in fear of slave revolt. Elites in both colonies enjoyed phenomenal wealth that enabled them to live splendidly in the English manner and to build elaborate public buildings, private houses, and showy cultural institutions, while at least the wealthiest among them even managed altogether to escape the unhealthy disease environment that characterized both colonies.

If, however, the parallels were so striking, how do we explain why in the American Revolution Jamaica stayed within the British Empire, while South Carolina joined the other continental colonies in revolt? This question becomes more salient when we realize that the Jamaican Assembly in 1774 petitioned the Crown endorsing the American arguments against the Coercive Acts and other measures that led directly to the Revolution but indicating that its enormous population of slaves made it too weak to offer any physical resistance.[20] We may search for the answers to this puzzle in South Carolina's continental situation or in the many ways it had fallen short of Jamaica in realizing the full potential of the Barbados model in a larger physical setting. South Carolina did not have such a large or disproportionately black and slave population as did Jamaica, it had not had nearly so much overt slave unrest, and it had far less absenteeism and, perhaps, a white settler elite that was considerably more committed to maintaining its ties with the colony. Notwithstanding these important differences, however, South Carolina did have a lot of slaves, and in 1775-76 it was, in fact, nearly paralyzed by the fear that if it carried resistance against Britain too far political chaos and slave revolt might follow.[21]

20 Jamaica Assembly's Petition to the King, Dec. 28, 1774, in Peter Force, ed., *American Archives* (Washington, D.C., 1837-53), 4th ser., I, pp. 1072-74; George Metcalf, *Royal Government and Political Conflict in Jamaica 1729-1783* (London, 1965), pp. 167- 91; Richard B. Sheridan, "The Jamaican Slave Insurrection Scare of 1776 and the American Revolution," *Journal of Negro History* LXI (1976): 199-301.

21 See Robert Olwell, "Domestick Enemies: Slavery and Political Independence in South Carolina" (unpublished seminar paper, Johns Hopkins University, 1985).

John Drayton, one of South Carolina's earliest social analysts, had, perhaps, a better answer to this question. During the twenty years before the Revolution, Drayton observed in his *View of South Carolina,* published in 1802, the wholesale influx of white settlers into the backcountry of South Carolina "added thousands to her domestic strength." That influx, which raised the colony's white population from 25,000 in 1750 to 87,000 in 1780, was by the mid-1770s slowly altering South Carolina's racial composition. Instead of 2 to 1, the proportion of black slaves to white free people was falling to 1.1 to 1, almost to parity. Only with the augmentation of her "domestic strength" in the form of growing numbers of whites, Drayton implied, did South Carolina have the wherewithal even to begin "collecting and preparing against a revolution." Without that vast immigration, Drayton thus suggested, South Carolina would have found it impossible to revolt—for the very same reason that deterred Jamaica. According to Drayton, this was the critical social fact that gave lowcountry South Carolina leaders the nerve to revolt.[22]

Of course, it was a social fact that obtained only temporarily. As soon as backcountry planters could secure the capital to buy slaves, they did so, and the successful introduction of cotton culture into the area in the 1780s and 1790s greatly accelerated the process. In a very real sense, the spread of cotton and slavery across the Lower South over the next half century testified to the continuing viability and adaptability of the Barbadian social model.

That model had not, in any case, ever been confined by national boundaries. Already by the late seventeenth century, it was being successfully adapted by the French in the small islands of Guadeloupe and Martinique. During the following century, it would be established, again by the French, in the large island colony of St. Domingue. In the nineteenth century, it was extended to the Spanish islands of Cuba and Puerto Rico. In the 1790s, the continuing affinity of lowcountry South Carolina with the West Indies was pointedly underlined by the ease with which the many refugees from the St. Domingue revolt, the only genuine social revolution to take place during the so-called era of democratic revolutions, were first welcomed by and then settled happily into lowcountry society.

22 John Drayton, *View of South Carolina* (Charleston, 1802), pp. 102-03.

Review of *The Barbados-Carolina Connection*

BY WARREN ALLEYNE AND HENRY FRASER. LONDON: MACMILLAN CARIBBEAN, 1988. PP. VI, 74. UNAVAILABLE FOR SALE IN THE UNITED STATES (COPY CAN BE CONSULTED AT SOUTH CAROLINA HISTORICAL SOCIETY LIBRARY) (PAPER).

Originally published in Volume 92, Number 1 (January 1991)

This attractively produced volume is a tribute to the long connection between Barbados and Carolina. In 1985, the two authors came to South Carolina as a result of an opportunity afforded by the Barbados Board of Tourism. One of the reviewers, at that time chairman of the Department of History at the University of South Carolina, entertained the Barbadian delegation. Friendships were forged. In June 1989, George Rogers and George and Harriet Williams visited Barbados for the first time. To their surprise they were met at the airport by Warren Alleyne and Henry Fraser, who presented them with copies of this recently published volume. The Barbados-Carolina connection has always flourished on the basis of these personal associations.

When Captain William Hilton set sail from Speightstown in 1663, he could not have known that he was establishing such a succession of fruitful associations. Henry Woodward, left behind in America by Captain Hilton, is the best example, for he found his way to Florida and back to the West Indies before returning to the mainland in the first fleet of 1670.

The successful production of sugar in Barbados at Drax Hall as early as 1640 and at St. Nicholas Abbey by the 1660s had pushed younger sons to look for new lands. When the first Draytons and Middletons arrived from Barbados in the late 1670s and acquired land on the Ashley River they were also casting lines to the future.

But the best example of a long-standing tie is Sir John Yeamans, who resided at St. Nicholas Abbey before moving to Carolina where he established himself near Goose Creek on land which is still known as Yeamans Hall. The authors capture these interconnected threads by portraying on the cover of the volume St. Nicholas Abbey and Middleton Place. Sugar and rice were the two great staples. The 1989 visitors to St. Nicholas Abbey were privileged to see women winding their way homeward through the fields of sugar cane with burdens on their heads as they and their ancestors before them had been wont to do for over 300 years. The present owner of the estate told the visitors that the culture of sugar cane would not last beyond the present generation.

The authors record that they met in Carolina one of the descendants of a slave who came with the first Drayton. "[T]he gatekeeper at Drayton Hall, 70 year old Richmond Bowen, claims to be an eighth generation descendant of a slave named

Bowen who accompanied Thomas Drayton. (The name Bowen is strongly associated with the parish of St. Lucy in Barbados.)"

Barbados had been laid out in six parishes; South Carolina in 1706 in ten, the names of some of the latter being taken from the names of the former. As William Gilmore Simms afterwards wrote, parish society was all-important in the early development of Carolina and the model of the plantation complex came from Barbados.

The good and the evil that flowed from the island to the continent were as inexorably intertwined as wealth and slavery. Stede Bonnet of Christ Church Parish, Barbados, the most notable pirate in Carolina history, was convicted of piracy and hanged at Oyster Point.

The transfer of language and of house styles illustrates the transfer of culture from the island to the mainland. The chapter on "Gullah and Bajun Dialect" shows the many similarities between the speech patterns of the islanders and of the Afro-American residents of coastal South Carolina. Though these parallels are well worth drawing, Dr. Fraser might profitably have extended his study to include the speech patterns of the non-Gullah-speaking residents of the area. The late Samuel G. Stoney some fifty years ago used to assert that there were five distinct dialects in Charleston. Though that richness of variety has passed away, it is true that some non-Gullah speakers a generation ago used the palatalized "c" and "g" still common in Barbados (as in "kyar" and "gyarden"), and it is still standard to hear in Charleston the diphthongized "a" and "o" (as in "layut" [late] and "bo-ut" [boat]) that mark some Bajun speakers. This chapter does not provide so thorough an account of its subject as the other chapters do of theirs, but it says enough for the purposes of this book.

One of the most intriguing chapters is Dr. Fraser's account of the connection with Charleston in architecture. The origin of the Charleston single house, unique to the city and seldom seen elsewhere in Carolina, is obscure, but Dr. Fraser is entirely correct in saying that oral tradition traces it to the West Indies and often, particularly, to Barbados. In investigating this tradition, he is the first to have seriously treated the comments of the seventeenth-century observer, Richard Ligon, in his *True and Exact History of the Island of Barbados* (published in London in 1657), which are closely keyed to the relationship between climate and domestic building. Carl and Roberta Bridenbaugh, indeed, cited Ligon's *True and Exact History* in their valuable *No Peace Beyond the Line*, but their view, being northeastern, was limited; they emphasized the exotic house (T-shaped) that Ligon proposed to build. Dr. Fraser, being southeastern, has grappled more vigorously with Ligon's analysis of domestic architecture; he emphasizes the standard Barbadian house form that Ligon proposed to improve.

In his earlier book, *Historic Houses of Barbados*, Dr. Fraser mentioned Ligon's importance to Barbados and Charleston architecture, but in the work under review he observes further that Ligon uses the terms "single house" and "double house" "in a way that has survived in Charleston and [in] Charleston alone." This is, perhaps, to overstate. Ligon does not define what he means by "single house"; and as his "double house" describes a structure very different from the form that that term defines in Charleston—and elsewhere—we must approach both terms with skepticism. Nevertheless, as the *Oxford English Dictionary* records the first use of "single house" in English in Sir Walter Scott's *The Heart of Midlothian* in 1818, Dr. Fraser's discovery of that term in Ligon in 1657 will undoubtedly generate much discussion. And so it should.

Ligon uses the term "double house" to describe a house roofed with two parallel pitched-roof systems, the gutter between them running parallel to the long axis of the roofs, a style still represented in its simplest form in the "chattel house" in Barbados. The entrance to such houses tends to be centered in the wall of the house that is parallel to the ridgepole of the roof. The term "single house," as Scott uses it, would seem to refer to a house having a single room on each floor with an exterior staircase to the rooms on the upper storeys. Though Ligon is not specific, he might have been referring in his use of the term to such a single-roomed house, i.e., a half of a double house, for in describing his own "ideal" double house, Ligon seems to think of it as basically a two-roomed house—though, in his plan, covered with a single roof—not the double roof that characterized the other double houses of the island.

Since Ligon has not, in fact, defined what he means by "single house," it is perhaps too hasty of Dr. Fraser to say that Ligon has used the term in a way that has survived in Charleston. There is a difference in perspective: in Barbados the main entry to the single house would seem to be centered in the long side of the house, the house being conceived as fronting on that side as indeed are the plantation houses cited here—Brighton House (1652), the Principal's Lodge, Codrington College (c. 1670 or earlier), and the Bay Mansion (of uncertain date). In Charleston, the main entry would seem to be in the short side, the house being conceived as fronting on that side. The earliest single houses in Charleston have an entrance in the short side, fronting on the street, with a supplementary entrance in the long side. In later times, the entrance in the short side moves to the piazza end of the street front where it serves as an access to the supplementary entry in the long side; later still, the entrance in the short side moves to the opposite end of the street front and the supplementary entry disappears.

Dr. Fraser's thesis is that Ligon's proposals for Barbados design influenced the design of the Charleston single house; the evidence supporting this thesis is historical, linguistic, pictorial, and architectural. The historical evidence points to the connections between the two colonies which are well documented, not least in the first chapters of this book, which are based upon Warren Alleyne's vast knowledge of the island. The linguistic evidence displayed here is intriguing; the pictorial evidence is the 1695 engraving of Bridgetown by Samuel Copen; and the architectural evidence consists of the structures still surviving on Barbados from the seventeenth to the early eighteenth centuries. These last two types of evidence are ambiguous. In the engraving there are, in fact, structures that can be described as "tall, narrow, gabled houses...standing close but separate"—like Charleston houses; there are also what seem to be both row houses and double houses (in Ligon's sense of the term). Of these structures, none remains today in identifiable shape. Furthermore, though he was true and exact in many details, Copen pictures Bridgetown as a cluster of houses with many chimneys. More chimneys, it would seem, than would be necessary for kitchens. Is it likely that so many houses were still in 1695 being built with chimneys that would never be used? Is it possible that Copen was generalizing?

Of survivals elsewhere on the island cited by Dr. Fraser, not all are equally convincing as originals of the single-house design. Three of these are the plantation houses already noted, and though they are "built longwise," they are scarcely models for the single-house urban dwelling that Kenneth Severens has aptly described in *Charleston Antebellum Architecture and Civic Destiny* as a sensitive compromise "between the public need for urban density and the private need for domestic seclusion." Dr. Fraser stresses the fact that these three are, as Ligon stipulated, built "upon an East and West line," an orientation that has been held traditionally to be a determinant of a Charleston single house in its purest form. Gene Waddell, however, has argued that this characteristic is not an essential ("The Charleston Single House," *Preservation Progress*, March 1977 [Vol. 22, No. 2]); many of the most typical Charleston houses are not so oriented.

The Seaview Hotel in Hastings (a "suburb" of Bridgetown) would seem to be a mixed example. It is built long-wise, but its proportion is three-to-two (sixty feet in depth; forty feet in breadth along the street), a handsome classic proportion not standard in Charleston where the single house tends to be attenuated and narrow. The entrance is in the middle of the long side: it leads to a central hall and to a stairway to the upper floor, but the disposition of the ground-floor rooms is altogether different from that of a Charleston house. Somewhat disconcerting to Dr. Fraser's thesis is the fact that the building does not have the gable end on the narrow side; instead, the roof of the structure follows Ligon's description of a double house, with "a double cover, that is, two gable ends, and a gutter between." The building might be equally well described as one of Ligon's double houses with the entrance misplaced (it is in the side of the house that is at right angels to the ridgepole).

The urban examples that have survived from Bridgetown and from Speightstown are more convincing examples of Barbados originals. The example from Speightstown, "Arlington," as Dr. Fraser correctly notes, "could have come straight out of Copen's engraving and shows a remarkable resemblance to early Charleston houses." There are other instances, Dr. Fraser reports, in Bay Street and elsewhere, now considerably altered, but the Nicholls building in Lucas Street is perhaps the best example, and not simply because of its graceful gable.

However, one must wonder why, if a style was so common that it could be exported, so few examples of it remained at home. Dr. Fraser explains the losses as due to fire and hurricane. Charleston also has been visited by fire and hurricane (and by earthquake, too), yet many dwellings of this style remain from this period.

Dr. Fraser's enthusiasm, then, must be tempered with some caution. On the other hand, Gene Waddell's confidence that we can trace the beginnings of the Charleston single house without resorting to outside influences seems overly parochial. Ligon left Barbados, having failed (in three years) to persuade the settlers to build after his fashion; the adventurers came to Carolina to secure a way of life they could not secure on the island. It is certainly possible that Dr. Fraser is correct in encouraging us to believe that one of those things was a house properly constructed for the climate—long-wise, with its short end to the city street.

The extraordinarily beautiful illustrations emphasize the contrasts and clarify the arguments.

University of South Carolina — George C. Rogers, Jr.
Duke University — George W. Williams

The South Carolina Slave Laws Reconsidered, 1670-1700

THOMAS J. LITTLE
DOCTORAL CANDIDATE IN HISTORY, RICE UNIVERSITY

Originally published in Volume 94, No 2 (April 1993)

BY THE END OF THE SEVENTEENTH CENTURY THE SLAVE LAWS in South Carolina had assumed definite form. Modeled on statutes promulgated in Barbados, these laws were the most draconian on the English mainland. Although the slave laws did not mirror actual practice and were not always stringently enforced, they are a valuable source for investigating the early history of the colony, affording a clear though admittedly narrow window into the emerging slave society. The leading slaveholders who controlled the colonial assembly articulated their views on the necessities of the slave system in these statutes; therefore, the statutes may be analyzed profitably to explore, among other things, questions concerning the expectations, fears, and anxieties of the principal slaveowners, the master-slave relationship, the character of slavery, and the superstructure of control.[1] Together with a close analysis of the South Carolina slave laws from 1670 to 1700, this essay will attempt to place these laws firmly within their social, political, and economic contexts. This approach gives the laws added meaning and allows for a more nuanced exploration of their relationship to particular developments within the colony.[2]

1 William M. Wiecek, "The Statutory Law of Slavery and Race in the Thirteen Mainland Colonies of British America," *William and Mary Quarterly*, 3rd Ser., Vol. XXXIV (April 1977), pp. 258-280; Winthrop D. Jordan, *White Over Black: American Attitudes Toward the Negro*, 1550-1812 (Chapel Hill: University of North Carolina Press, 1968), pp. 587-588; Elsa V. Goveia, "The West Indian Slave Laws of the Eighteenth Century," *Rivista de Ciencias Sociales* 4 (March 1960), pp. 75-105.

2 Studies giving the South Carolina slave laws special attention include M. Eugene Sirmans, "The Legal Status of the Slave in South Carolina, 1670-1740," *Journal of Southern History* 28 (September 1962), pp. 462-473; A. Leon Higginbotham, Jr., *In the Matter of Color: Race and the American Legal Process, the Colonial Period* (New York: Oxford University Press,1978), pp. 151-215; Ed wa rd McCrady, "Slavery in th e Province of South Carolina, 1670-1770," in *Annual Report of the American Historical Association for the Year 1895* (Washington, D.C.: American Historical Association, 1896), pp. 631-673. Although the South Carolina slave laws have been the focus of a number of studies, our understanding of their underlying dimensions remains clouded. Part of the problem stems from a scholarly tendency to rely solely on compilations of the South Carolina acts of assembly published by the colonial and state governments. These compilations are more convenient to use than the main body of surviving statutes still in manuscript form at the South Carolina Department of Archives and History, but they can lead to errors in fact and interpretation because they omit important legislation. Charles M. Andrews, *The Colonial Period of American History* (New Haven: Yale University Press,1934-1938), Vol. III, pp. 183-187;Wesley Frank Craven, *The Colonies in Transition, 1660-1713* (New York: Harper and Row, 1968), pp. 42-43, 56-57, 97-99; Peter H. Wood, *Black Majority: Negroes in Colonial South Carolina from 1670 through the Stono Rebellion* (New York: Knopf, 1974), pp. 14-15.

The establishment and effective maintenance of slavery in South Carolina rested on the legality of slavery and on the assumption that masters had complete personal dominion over their bondspersons. All of the Carolina proprietors were fully aware of this fact. They were well-informed about colonial affairs and familiar with the institution of slavery. But if their settlement was to be successful they had to assure prospective colonists that their commitment to these fundamental aspects of the peculiar institution were genuine, especially since they expected to relocate experienced slave-owning West Indians to the Carolina coast. Thus the Fundamental Constitutions of Carolina, drafted in 1669, accepted and even encouraged the development of black slavery in the colony, granting every freeman "absolute Power and Authority over his Negro slaves, of what opinion or Religion soever." The word "power" was conspicuously added to the clause in one of the earliest revisions of the Constitutions and reflects an obvious attempt to quell any fears among prospective settlers—especially those from the West Indies—that their dominion over black slaves would be anything less than "absolute."[3]The proprietors knew that both power and authority would be essential to creating and maintaining a slave-based plantation society in the remote outback of the British Empire. Ultimately, however, it was the local slaveowners who determined how their "absolute Power and Authority" would be exercised. South Carolina's Caribbean roots are thus of primary importance. As a number of scholars have shown, Barbadians played a determinative role in the early history of South Carolina.[4]

3 Mattie Erma Edwards Parker, ed., *North Carolina Charters and Constitutions, 1578-1698* (Raleigh, N.C.: Carolina Charter Tercentennary Commission, 1963), pp. 150,164,183. In contemporary usage, "authority" connotedrulebyconsent;itrelied on willing obedience, deference, and respect. "Power," on the other hand, was synonymous with force, compulsion, and might; it meant, as Bernard Bailyn has shown, "the dominion of some men over others, the human control of human life." For a discussion of the meaning of "power" and"authority" in thecontext of an early modem British worldview see Jack P. Greene, "Independence, Improvement, and Authority: Toward a Framework for Understanding the Histories of the Southern Backcountry during theEra of the American Revolution," in Ronald Hoffman, Thad W. Tate, and Peter J. Albert, eds., *An Uncivil War: The Southern Backcountry during the American Revolution* (Charlottesville: University Press of Virginia, 1985), pp. 3-36; and Bernard Bailyn, *The Ideological Origins of the American Revolution* (Cambridge, Mass.: BelknappPressforHarvard University Press, 1967), pp. 55-93,56(quotation).

4 The South Carolina-Caribbean connection may be followed in Richard S. Dunn, "The English Sugar Islands and the Founding of South Carolina," *South Carolina Historical Magazine* (hereafter *SCHM)* 72 (April 1971), pp. 81 -93; Richard Waterhouse, "England, the Caribbean, and the Founding of South Carolina," *Journal of American Studies* 9 (December 1975), pp. 259-281; John P. Thomas Jr., "The Barbadians in Early South Carolina," *SCHM* 31 (April 1930), pp. 75-92; Peter H. Wood, *Black Majority,* passim; Converse D. Clowse, *Eco,wmic Beginnings in Colonial South Carolina, 1670-1730* (Columbia: University of South Carolina Press, 1971), passim. For South Carolina's continuing connection to the Caribbean see Jack P. Greene, "Colonial South Carolina and the Caribbean Connection," *SCHM* 88, (December 1987), pp. 192-210; Warren Alleyne and Henry Fraser, *The Barbado sCarolina Connection* (London: Macmillan Caribbean, 1988).

ABOUT ONE-HALF OF THE WHITES WHO EMIGRATED TO THE colony between 1670 and 1690 came from Barbados. The majority of these whites were from the small-planter and freemen classes—a small planter being classified as one owning at least ten acres of land but less than twenty slaves and a freeman as one owning less than ten acres. However, recent work has suggested that a significant number of whites from the big- and middling-planter classes immigrated to the colony—a big planter being classified as one owning sixty or more slaves and a middling planter as one owning between twenty and fifty-nine slaves.[5] Similarly, Richard Waterhouse has identified representatives of at least thirty-three middling Barbadian planter families who immigrated to the colony during the first two decades of settlement.[6]

These Barbadians had a strong preference for African slave labor and introduced the institution of slavery into South Carolina. Most of the slaves who came into the colony during the initial phase of settlement also came from the West Indies, especially from Barbados. In fact, Barbados was South Carolina's chief source of black labor during the seventeenth century. While no reliable population statistics are available before 1700, Peter Wood has suggested "that even in the earliest years, between one fourth and one third of the colony 's newcomers were Negroes."[7] This distribution seems to have lasted for the first two decades of settlement. (See Table 1.)

TABLE I

Estimated Population of South Carolina, 1675–1710*

Year	White	Black	Total
1675	375-400	125-150	500-600
1680	750-900	250-300	1,000-1,200
1685	1,875-2,025	625-675	2,500-2,700
1690	2,500	1,100	3,600
1703	3,800	3,000	6,800
1708	4,080	4,100	8,180

*Clowse, *Economic Beginnings*, pp. 251-252; Wood, *Black Majority*, pp. 21-24, 144

5 These social classifications are drawn from Dunn, "The Barbados Census of 1680: Profile of the Richest Colony in English America," *William and Mary Quarterly*, 3rd Ser., Vol. XXVI (January, 1969), pp. 11-12. Richard Dunn has shown, for example, that representatives of at least eighteen big-planter families from Barbados obtained land in Carolina between 1670 and 1692. See Dunn, "The English Sugar Islands," p. 84.

6 Waterhouse, "England, the Caribbean, and the Founding of South Carolina," p. 273.

7 Wood, *Black Majority*, p p. 14-62, 25 (quotation).

But population estimates tend to obscure important local differences. Large numbers of slaves were owned by a few Barbadian planters living on remote tracts of land. Sir John Yeamans, a prominent Barbadian who served as governor of South Carolina from 1672 to 1674, for instance, lived on an isolated barony worked by more than twenty-six slaves.[88] The sparse pattern of settlement in the colony and the apparent emptiness of the countryside must have led contemporary observers to underestimate the number of slaves living and working on these island baronies. Therefore, although slaves accounted for only one-quarter to one-third of the total population before 1690, in certain peripheral areas they probably held a clear majority. South Carolina's ties with the Caribbean were reinforced by commercial transactions. Carolinians shipped lumber, pipe staves, pitch, tar, resin, beef, pork, corn, peas, and Indian slaves to the West Indies in exchange for sugar, black slaves, and various other commodities, such as salt and fruit.[9] Stated simply, trade connected the two regions; it established important linkages between families, friends, relatives, and associates. This continuous flow of goods and people facilitated an interchange of news and ideas. One aspect of that interchange proved to be particularly troubling to South Carolina's slaveowners: news of slave rebellion in the West Indies.[10] Reports were not infrequent. Numerous slave conspiracies were uncovered in Barbados during the seventeenth century and in 1687 there was a major uprising in Antigua. Jamaica, characteristically wracked by rebellion, reported at least six sizable slave revolts between 1673 and 1694.[11] This news constantly reminded white Carolinians of their potential domestic enemies and provided an alarming backdrop against which all slave laws were passed in South Carolina during the seventeenth century.

8 Governor West to Lord Ashley, September 1, 1671, in Langdon Cheves, ed., *The Shaftesbury Papers and Other Records Relating to Carolina and the First Settlement on the Ashley River Prior to the Year 1676*, in *Collection s of the South Carolina Hi storical Society* (Charleston: South Carolina Historical Society, 1897), Vol. V, p. 337 (hereafter cited as Cheves, ed., *Shaftesbury Papers).*

9 Clowse, *Economic Beginnings*, pp. 1-138; John J. McCusker and Russell R. Menard, *The Economy of British America, 1607-1789* (Chapel Hill: University of North Carolina Press, 1985), pp. 144-188.

10 Greene, "Colonial South Carolina and the Caribbean Connection," pp. 199-201.

11 Hilary Beckles, *Black Rebellion in Barbados: The Struggle Against Slavery* (Bridgetown, Barbados: Carib Research and Publications, 1984), pp. 41-48; Dunn, *Sugar and Slaves: The Rise of the Planter Class in the English West Indies, 1624-1714* (Chapel Hill: University of North Carolina Press, 1972), pp. 256-262; Orlando Patterson, *The Sociology of Slavery* (London: MacGibbon and Kee, 1967), p. 267.

DURING THE FIRST DECADE OF SETTLEMENT, SOUTH CAROLINIANS were afforded a great deal of local independence. Barbadians dominated the colonial government and attempted to resist the restraints and policies imposed from outside. The settlers adapted their economic activities to the wilderness environment, devoting themselves to livestock, provisions, minor staples, the Indian trade, and the provisioning of pirates.[12] Slaves were employed in all of these diverse economic activities and were afforded a small degree of individual autonomy. In South Carolina, where there was an abundance of land, it was common to allocate slaves small provision grounds and a certain amount of time to cultivate them. This practice was predominant in the West Indies, especially in Jamaica. These provision grounds were usually located at some distance from the slaves' living quarters and should not be confused with the so-called garden plots. Normally, slaves worked about one acre of land and grew corn, beans, peas, potatoes, and yams; in addition, slaves sometimes owned or co-owned hogs, cows, goats, chickens, or cordwood. The provision ground system had a number of advantages in the far-distant periphery of the British world. First, slaves could provide all of their own food—the most costly of all slave maintenance expenditures in an infant economy. Second, masters could purchase any excesses grown by their slaves at a much reduced rate; in turn, they could make a profit by selling these goods on the open market. Finally, the provision grounds acted as a method of social control. They gave slaves a vested interest in the land and made them less likely to run away.[13] The provision-ground system, therefore, was an integral part of South Carolina's fragile society and economy during the initial phase of colonization.

Given the dominant influence of experienced Barbadian settlers in the early years, it is not surprising that the proprietors made a concerted effort to reassert their authority. In 1682 they twice revised the Fundamental

12 Sirmans, *Colonial South Carolina: A Political Hi story, 1663-1763* (Chapel Hill: University of North Carolina Press, 1966), pp. 19-34; Clowse, *Economic Beginnings*, pp. 42-94.

13 The provision-ground system in South Carolina is currently under investigation. See Philip D. Morgan, "Work and Culture: The Task System and the World of Low Country Blacks, 1700-1880," *William and Mary Quarterly*, 3rd Ser., Vol. XXXIX (October 1982), pp. 563-597. It has received more attention in the West Indies. This is especially true of Jamaica where there was a comparative abundance of land. See, for example; Patterson, *The Sociology of Slavery*, pp. 219-234; Sidney W. Mintz and Douglas Hall, "The Origins of the Jamaican Internal Marketing System," in Sidney W. Mintz, comp., *Papers in Caribbean Anthropology* (New Haven, Conn.: Yale University Press, 1960), pp. 13-17; Richard B. Sheridan, *Sugar and Slavery: An Economic History of the British West Indies, 1623-1775* (Baltimore: Johns Hopkins University Press, 1974), pp. 95, 259-260.

Constitutions and instituted various political, economic, and legal reforms in order to bring the colony under tighter control. They also launched a serious promotional campaign to recruit new settlers, not only to foster prosperity, but also to offset the unruly Barbadians. This recruiting drive attracted a number of diverse groups to the colony, including Huguenots, English Baptists, English and Scottish Presbyterians, and Quakers.[14] These dissenters, many of whom came to the colony as indentured servants, boosted the total population of South Carolina to 2,000 or 2,500 by 1685.[15] The proprietors' attempt to reassert their authority and the influx of dissenters combined to arouse an anti-proprietary faction in the colony. West Indian immigrants formed the power base of this group. Because many of them lived near Goose Creek, a small rivulet flowing into the Cooper River, they became known as the "Goose Creek men." Jealous of their local autonomy, the Goose Creek men viewed proprietary reform measures and the newly arrived dissenters with a jaundiced eye.[16] They believed that proprietary "innovations" represented an unwarranted abuse of power and they were determined to resist, oppose, or ignore these measures at every tum. As for the dissenters, the Goose Creek men saw them as meddling interlopers who, with the help of the proprietors, threatened to break their local power. Equally alarming was the fact that the new flood of white indentured servants began illicitly trading with slaves shortly after they arrived in the colony. The Goose Creek men believed that these illegal exchanges facilitated the planning of escapes, conspiracies, and other subversive deeds. Similarly, contraband trade seriously limited a master's ability to purchase excesses produced by his slaves, cutting into his profits, and undermining an important social-control measure.

With their personal authority over blacks threatened, the Goose Creek men used their political power to prevent alternative economic enterprises from encroaching on their control of the labor force. In September 1683 the colonial parliament passed an "Act Inhibiting the Trading between Servants

14 There is some question as to the effectiveness of proprietary promotional efforts in the 1680sand the relationship to the movement of people. Shaftesbury may have played a greater role in promoting newcomers than did promotionalliterature. See Hope Frances Kane, "Colonial Promotion and Promotion Literature of Carolina, 1660-1700" (Ph.D. dissertation, University of North Carolina, 1961), pp. 73-82; RobertM. Weir, *Colonial South Carolina: A History* (Millwood, N.Y.: KTOPress, 1983), pp. 62-65; Sirmans, *Colonial South Carolina,* pp. 36-37; Clowse, *Economic Beginnings,* pp. 72-75.

15 Clowse, *Economic Beginnings,* p. 74.

16 Sirmans, *Colonial South Carolina,* pp. 35-43.

and Slaves" to put a stop to illicit exchanges. Because many of the earliest statutes passed by the South Carolina legislature have not been preserved, this act exists in title only.[17] Nevertheless, the appearance of this law is symptomatic of the fears and anxieties of the ruling elites of the colony. Specifically, the statute reflects a determination of the colony's principal slaveowners—transplanted Barbadians—to reassert control. To them, day-to-day encounters between servants and slaves undermined established power relationships and commonly understood rules of conduct.

During the 1680s the colonial assembly increasingly became a cockpit in which the Goose Creek men struggled for control of the government. In an effort to break their local power, the proprietors appointed Landgrave Joseph Morton, a leader among the English dissenters who had migrated to the colony, as governor. It soon became clear, however, that Morton was no match for the experienced Goose Creek men. In 1684 the proprietors asked their governor, "Are you to govern the people, or the people you?"[18] Perhaps the proprietors were a bit unfair to Morton because he apparently did his best to advance their interests against a practiced group of slippery Barbadians who could "with a bole of punch get who they would Chosen of the parliament and afterwards who they would chosen of the grand Councell."[19]

Following his instructions, Governor Morton called on all the members of the parliament that met in 1685 to subscribe to the new Fundamental Constitutions which, it will be recalled, had been revised in 1682. Twelve of the representatives stubbornly refused to comply, arguing that they already had subscribed to those of 1669. Not surprisingly, all were members of the anti-proprietary faction. They believed that arbitrary changes in the Fundamental Constitutions were "contrary to the nature of a fundamentall sacred and unalterable law."[20] Because of their refusal to adhere to the revised Constitutions, these twelve members

17 Acts number 1 to number 22, extending from 1682 to 1685, have never been found, but titles do appear. See Thomas Cooper and David J. McCord, eds., *Statutes at Large of South Carolina,* Vol. II (Act no. 7) (Columbia, S.C.: A.S. Johnston, 1837), p.v. This has led several historians astray, believing there were no acts dealing with slavery before 1687. For example, see McCrady, "Slavery in the Province of South Carolina," p. 391; Morgan, "Work and Culture," p. 569; Clowse, *Economic Beginnings,* 106.

18 Quoted in William J. Rivers, *A Sketch of the History of South Carolina* (Charleston, S.C.: McCarter & Co, 1856; repr. Spartanburg, S.C.: The Reprint Co., 1972), p. 137.

19 Quoted in Sirmans, *Colonial South Carolina,* p. 38.

20 Quoted in Ibid., p. 44.

were excluded from officeholding. Every law passed during this session of parliament, therefore, was enacted by the remaining members, all of whom were proprietary supporters. Since statutes were normally to remain in force for a period of only twenty-three months, this skeleton assembly revived several laws that "by experience have been found very useful and much tending to the publick good thereof." Interestingly, the 1683 "Act Inhibiting Trading" was not revived, suggesting that those most concerned with the provision—the Goose Creek men—did not have a voice in the matter.[21]

PARTY STRIFE WAS SOON FORGOTTEN WHEN THE SPANISH launched a surprise attack on the exposed southern frontier in 1686. While moving toward Charleston, the invaders were forced to retreat after a hurricane ripped through their path. Nevertheless, the Spanish force managed to carry off ten slaves before heading home. A counter-attack was immediately planned by the Carolinians. Four hundred men were armed and two vessels were fitted out. This expedition was aborted when a new governor, James Colleton, arrived in the province. Colleton, who had recently come to the colony from Barbados, argued that the expedition could not be legally carried out because Spain had not formally declared war. To prevent another attack, he reopened communications with the governor of Florida and persuaded him to pay for the slaves who had been carried off.[22]

Although Colleton was from Barbados, he was a proprietary supporter; this quickly put him at odds with the Goose Creek men.[23] The new governor summoned his first parliament at the end of 1686. Once again, the body was dominated by members of the anti-proprietary faction. After bolstering the colony's defenses, members of the Carolina

21 "An Act for the Reviving of Several Acts of Parliament Heretofore made in this Parte of the Province of Carolina which Lyeth South and West from Cape Feare," Cooper and McCord, *Statutes at Large,* Vol. II (Act no. 28), p. 13.

22 Sirmans, *Colonial South Carolina,* pp. 44-45.

23 The Colletons, who were major sugar planters in Barbados, obtained huge land grants in South Carolina. Sir John Colleton was one of the eight Carolina proprietors and was, in large part, responsible for the first efforts to colonize South Carolina. Peter Colleton, his eldest son, inherited the vast majority of his father's wealth, including the proprietary share. Peter owned a large sugar plantation and more than 180 slaves. Peter's younger brother Thomas was also a leading figure in Barbados. The third brother, James, "had no fruitful role in Barbados, and could rise to no office higher than vestryman for the local parish. So he came to Carolina, took out extensive land grants, and served as governor of the colony from 1686 to 1690." Dunn, "The English Sugar Islands," p. 85.

parliament passed another "Act Inhibiting Trading between Servants and Slaves" in February 1687. It was probably similar, if not identical, to the previous act of 1683 which had expired.[24]

The rationale behind this law is revealed in the preamble. It states that "there hath beene of late several indirect bargaines between freemen, servants and slaves, amongst themselves, whereby some evilly disposed, have adventured privately to embezzle, wast and sell divers of their master's goods, to the impoverishing of their said masters and the nourishing and introducing of vice into this province." Therefore, the act forbade "any freeman or free woman, servant or slave, to buy, sell, barter, contract, bargain or exchange any manner of goods or commodities whatsoever, of, for, to, or with any servant or slave in this Province without the privity or consent of the masters." The 1686 act also sought to discourage trading between servants and slaves to rectify "divers other disorders and enormities" that it produced. Contagious in nature, it was believed that subversive activities facilitated by illicit trading had a tendency to infect the "more civilly minded servants and slaves" in the colony.[25]

The legislators drew up a series of penalties to discourage this practice. Free persons who were found buying goods from or selling goods to servants or slaves without the consent of the masters were to "pay ten times the real value... to the person whose goods were soe sold and disposed." A servant or slave found guilty of the same crime would "suffer and abide such punishment or censure, not extending to the taking away life or limb." Indentured servants "so offending in any manner as aforesaid, shall, after the expiration of their term of servitude, serve so long time to his master or mistresse...as any three Justices of the Peace

24 Cooper and McCord, *Statutes at Large, Vol. II* (Act no. 34), pp. 22-23. Many historians have failed to recognize that the early statutes were recorded according to the civil year, which did not commence until March 25. The historical year began on January 1. In other words, this act, which was ratified on February 26 in the civil year 1686, was actually passed in the historical year 1687. This has led several scholars to mistakenly date the passage of this act as 1686. See, for example, Morgan, "Work and Culture," p. 569; Higginbotham, *In the Matter of Color*, p. 157; McCrady, "Slavery in the Province of South Carolina," pp. 633-634. I assume that the1687 "Act Inhibiting Trading" was similar to the previous act of 1683. A careful reading of all such acts passed between 1670 and 1700. See Cooper and McCord, *Statutes at Large, Vol. II* (Act no. 34), pp. 22-23, (Act no. 60), pp. 52-54, and Governor Archdale's Law [1696], South Carolina Department of Archives and History, Columbia, S.C., (Act no. 135), pp. 28-30. Cooper and McCord failed to include act number 135 in their compilation. Nevertheless, all of these acts are almost identical and do not reveal any significant change over time.

25 Cooper, *Statutes at Large, Vol. I* (Act no. 34) (Columbia, S.C.: A.S. Johnston, 1836), p. 22.

shall judge convenient to make satisfaction for the value and loss of such goods."This last provision, of course, did not apply to slaves because they were held in bondage for life. One of the most important features of this law was the restriction of slave mobility. In contrast to white servants, slaves were always required to carry passes when venturing outside the limits of their farm or plantation.

The act stated:

> It shall not be lawful for any negroe or negroes... upon any pretence whatsoever to travel or goe abroad, from his or their master or mistresses house in the night time, between the sunsetting and the sun-rising, or in the day time, without a note from his or their master or mistresse or overseer.

The law also empowered any person—black or white—to "reasonably... chastise and correct" any slave found to be in violation of the rule.[26]

This piece of legislation was passed soon after news reached South Carolina that Barbadian planters had uncovered a conspiracy between Irish servants and African slaves. After investigating the plot, twenty slaves were found guilty and brutally executed. South Carolinians also received news reports that more than twenty-five whites had been killed in a devastating year-long rebellion in Jamaica during 1685 and 1686.[27]

As evidenced by the 1687 "Act Inhibiting Trading," Carolina slaveowners, speaking through the colonial assembly, were increasingly becoming concerned with the activities of the unfree labor force. Their opportunities for expressing their concern, however, were limited by the intense political factionalism plaguing the colony. The power struggle continued, and in the summer of 1687 the debate over the revised Fundamental Constitutions finally came to a head. After hearing that the proprietors had "utterly denyed" the Fundamental Constitutions of July 1669, "declaringe them to be but a Cappy of an imperfect Originall, & much more," the Goose Creek men openly challenged the legitimacy of the colonial government. They argued that the only legal foundation upon which the government was based was the royal charter granted

26 Ibid., *Vol. II* (Act no. 34), pp. 22-23.

27 Beckles, *Black Rebellion in Barbados,* pp. 41-42; D lll1ll, *Sugar and Slaves,* pp. 260-261.

to the proprietors in 1665.[28] Responding to this recalcitrance, Governor Colleton dissolved the assembly and refused to call another parliament for the rest of his tenure.

During the ensuing three-and-one-half year political deadlock, the situation in the colony became increasingly confused and unsettled. News reports of slave resistance in the sugar islands continued to haunt slaveowners in South Carolina, constantly reminding them of their potential domestic enemies.[29] Moreover, a minister was found to be "preaching a seditious sermon" in Charleston. This enthusiastic preacher, probably a Quaker or Baptist, was fined £100 and imprisoned until he came up with enough money to pay the prohibitive penalty.[30]

THESE TROUBLING EVENTS WERE SET AGAINST NEWS OF THE Glorious Revolution in England and reports of the rebellious actions taken in Massachusetts, New York, and Maryland. If that were not enough, there were rumors of a French invasion of the colony. Shortly after the outbreak of King William's War (1689-1697), the French seized the island of St. Christopher. South Carolinians feared they would be the next target of the French forces positioned in the Caribbean. Because the local government was at a standstill, the colonists could not prepare themselves for the seemingly imminent attack. Rather than calling an assembly to reenact important statutes that were beginning to expire, including laws concerning the internal and external defense of the colony, Governor Colleton, without the consent of the Goose Creek men, proclaimed martial law in 1690. As a result, the colony came to the brink of open rebellion.[31] Suddenly, Seth Sothel, one of the eight Carolina proprietors, arrived in the colony. Despite their objections to the Fundamental Constitutions, members of the anti-proprietary faction embraced Sothel who, as a proprietor, superseded Colleton as governor. As soon as a parliament was summoned, the Goose Creek men excluded

28 Address to Seth Sothel, 1690, in Rivers, *A Sketch of the History of South Carolina,* p. 419 (quotation); Sirmans, *Colonial South Carolina,* p. 46.

29 Between 1685 and 1688, for example, at least fifty-two slaves were executed for rebellious behavior in Barbados. Similar news came from the Leeward Islands and Jamaica. Beckles, *Black Rebellion in Barbados,* p. 42; Dunn, *Sugar and Slaves,* pp. 256-261.

30 Lords Proprietors to James Colleton, December, 2, 1689 in Rivers, *A Sketch of the History of South Carolina,* p. 410.

31 Sirmans, *Colonial South Carolina,* pp. 45 -49.

a number of proprietary supporters from political office and banished Colleton from the province.[32]

Shortly after the Barbadians regained power, a sweeping "Act for the Better Ordering of Slaves" was passed on February 7, 1691.[33] Modeled on laws passed by the Barbadian assembly in 1661, 1676, 1682, and 1688, this slave code reflects an increasing uneasiness among South Carolina slaveowners, especially after the turbulent events of the late 1680s. Since all acts relating to slaves rested on the basic assumption that slaves were property, this law stipulated that "as to payment of debts, [slaves] shall be deemed and taken as all other goods and chattels...and all negroes and slaves shall be accounted as freehold in all other cases whatsoever, and descend accordingly."[34] Simply put, as freehold property a slave was subject to the laws of inheritance; as chattel property they could be used in the payment of debts. This is an interesting distinction that reflects the influence of Barbadian slave codes, but many historians have been overly preoccupied with the legal status of slaves in South Carolina.[35] A slave's legal status did not affect his or her day-to-day existence. As Elsa Goveia has shown, what was of central importance to slaveholders in the statutory slave laws was that "it had to be made clear that the slave was property and subject to police regulations...which lay at the very heart of the slave system."[36] In other words, without police regulations the system of slavery could not have been maintained.

The South Carolina legislators who composed the 1691 code, therefore, were primarily concerned with police regulations—not the legal status of slaves. The law required masters to give slaves who ventured outside the limits of the plantation "a ticket, or one or more white men in their company; in which ticket shall be expressed their names and numbers, and also, from and to what place they are intended for, and time." The penalty for neglecting this responsibility was "forty shillings, and paying for taking up such slave as

32 Cooper and McCord, *Statutes at Large, Vol. II* (Acts no. 53 and no. 54), pp. 44- 46; Sirmans, *Colonial South Carolina*, pp. 49-50.

33 McCord, *Statutes at Large, Vol. VII* (Columbia, S.C.: A.S. Johnston, 1840), (Act no. 57), pp. 343-347. To my knowledge all scholars who have studied the South Carolina slave laws have mistakenly dated the passage of this law as 1690 because they have failed to differentiate between the civil and historical year. See, for example, Sirmans, "The Legal Status of the Slave in South Carolina," pp. 465-466; Wiecek, "The Statutory Law of Slavery and Race," p. 260; Wood, *Black Majority*, pp. 5-52.

34 McCord, *Statutes at Large, Vol. VII* (Act no 57), p. 343.

35 Sirmans, "The Legal Status of the Slave in South Carolina," pp. 462-473.

36 Goveia, "The West Indian Slave Laws of the Eighteenth Century," p. 82.

a runaway." For stealing a slave or harboring a runaway, whites were to be fined £60, convicted of a felony, and "excluded from the benefit of his clergy." Planters were expected to search slave quarters for weapons or stolen goods once every month. If a master killed a slave while administering punishment for some disorderly offense, the code proclaimed that "No person should be liable to the law for the same." However, if someone "out of wilfulness, wantoness, or bloody mindedness, shall kill a slave," he could be sentenced to three months in prison, without bail, and fined £50 (£10 less than for *stealing* a slave!).[37] Because slaves were considered property, the statute stated that masters were to be compensated by the government if their slaves were officially sentenced to death. Governmental compensation, of course, reduced the willingness of owners to conceal criminal slaves.[38]

Slave crime and punishment is clearly outlined in the 1691 code. For striking a white, slaves were subject to whipping, branding, nose slitting, and emasculation. If a slave ran away, he or she faced a "moderate whipping." Capital crimes included murder, rape, arson, assault, theft, preparation of offensive weapons, conspiracies, and rebellion. Under this law, slaves were tried for minor offenses by their masters and for major offenses by three freeholders and a justice of the peace.[39] Taken together, these policing measures provided an indirect justification for brutality. A master could severely discipline his slave knowing that he was acting within the law.

Interestingly, the 1691 act attempted to regulate further the economic activities of slaves by forbidding masters from dismissing their slaves from work on Saturday afternoon "as hath been accustomed formerly." This clause supplemented, but did not supersede, the "Act Inhibiting Trading between Servants and Slaves" which was passed again in March 1691.[40] In practice, the economic regulations, like the policing measures, were not always strictly enforced. It appears, for example, that slaves, being vigilant in defense of their customary privileges, were still afforded an opportunity to grow a wide range of provisions. Although these laws were not always enforced, and in many cases became nothing more than dead letters, they enabled masters to

37 McCord, *Statutes at Large, Vol. VII* (Act no. 57), p. 343 (first and second quotations), p. 345 (third quotation), p. 346 (fourth and fifth quotations).

38 Jordan, *White over Black*, p. 106.

39 McCord, *Statutes at Large, Vol. VII* (Act no. 57), pp. 343, 345-346.

40 Ibid., (Act. no. 57), p. 347 (quotation); *Vol. II* (Act no. 60), pp. 52-53.

limit the economic opportunities open to slaves in times of perceived danger or when the slaves' economic activities appeared to disrupt the social order.

When the other proprietors heard news of Sothel's actions, they suspended him from office. Subsequently, they appointed Philip Ludwell, who had served as the chief executive of North Carolina from 1689 to 1691, as governor. The proprietors instructed Ludwell to disallow all laws passed during Sothel's administration, to remove the Goose Creek men from office, and to reinstate those who had been displaced. Then they suspended the Fundamental Constitutions in an attempt to bring an end to the intense factionalism in the colony. Ludwell issued writs for a new parliament which met in June of 1692, but the council and assembly could not agree on anything.[41]

In the spring of 1693 the proprietors replaced Governor Ludwell with Landgrave Thomas Smith, a wealthy dissenter, because of the former's inability to deal with the Goose Creek men. Although Governor Smith enjoyed a relatively quiet administration, deep-rooted fissures still existed in the colony. The new governor recommended that a proprietor be sent to the province "with full power to heal their grievances."[42]

During Governor Smith's administration, the assembly twice reenacted both of the aforementioned acts relating to slaves. This systematic recapitulation of the slave laws demonstrates how completely the lives of the most notable slaveowners, speaking through the colonial assembly, were coming to be dominated by the perceived need to protect their interests and to control their bondspersons.[43] Frightening news from the West Indies continued to reach South Carolina. In the summer of 1692 a major slave conspiracy was uncovered in Barbados. It was believed that the slaves there had secretly formed six regiments and were planning to

41 Sirmans, *Colonial South Carolina,* pp. 49-53.

42 Quoted in Rivers, *A Sketch of the History of South Carolina,* p. 72.

43 Cooper and McCord, *Statutes at Large, Vol. II* (Acts nos. 101, 117, and 123), pp. viii, 78, 94, 96. Acts numbers 101 and 123 have not been preserved. Eugene Sirmans thought that "the only slave law enacted in South Carolina prior to 1696 had been passed in 1690 by Seth Sothel's assembly." This led him to conclude that "South Carolina did not yet really need a slave law as slaveholding was not to become widespread until about five years later, when the colony began to produce a marketable staple that required a large labor force." Sirmans, *Colonial South Carolina,* p. 64 (first quotation), Sirmans, "The Legal Status of the Slave in South Carolina," p. 465 (second quotation). A close examination of the statutes, however, reveals that the 1691 "Act for the Better Ordering of Slaves," (which Sirmans mistakenly dated 1690), together with an "Act Inhibiting Trading," was reinstated in 1693 and 1695.

capture the fortifications, burn the capital, and murder all the whites on the island. Two or three hundred slaves were arrested and 114 were executed.[44]

Interestingly, in 1693, the South Carolina Commons House of Assembly considered prohibiting the importation "of such slaves as have been conserned in any plott in Barbados."[45] The proprietors responded to Governor Smith's request and in the fall of 1695 John Archdale, one of the eight Carolina proprietors, arrived in the colony with extraordinary powers to appease the discontented settlers. Archdale spent several months "allaying the heats" of the colonists before he called his first parliament.[46] With conciliatory expressions to all parties, Governor Archdale was able to make conclusive a harmonious relationship between the two political factions. The parliament that convened in January 1696 passed a series of laws, known as Archdale's Laws, which came to be accepted generally by the colonists as part of the basic law of the province. Through compromise, Archdale was able to deal with some of the salient issues in the colony.[47]

The 1696 "Act for the Better Ordering of Slaves," passed during the administration of Archdale, represents the most forceful legislative statement concerning slavery on the English colonial mainland during the seventeenth century. The new South Carolina code drew heavily from the previous act of 1691, keeping in place many of the same policing measures. It also embraced more fully the Barbadian slave codes.[48] The preamble, for example, was borrowed directly from the Barbadian slave code of 1688. Similarly, clauses dealing with the trial of rebellious slaves and the dispersing of potentially dangerous gatherings on Sundays were drawn from the most up-to-date Barbadian statute.[49] The South Carolina assembly also enacted another economic-control measure to supplement the police law.[50] Both economic regulation and policing measures were becoming more and more essential as the number of slaves in the colony

44 Beckles, *Black Rebellion in Barbados*, pp. 41-48; Dunn, *Sugar and Slaves*, pp. 257-258.

45 A.S. Salley, Jr., ed., *Journal of the Commons House of Assembly of South Carolina*, 1693 (Columbia, S.C.: The State Company for the Historical Commission of South Carolina, 1907), p. 15.

46 Quoted in Rivers, *A Sketch of the History of South Carolina*, p. 180.

47 Sirmans, *Colonial South Carolina*, pp. 61-67.

48 Governor Archdale's Laws [1696], South Carolina Department of Archives and History, Columbia, S.C., pp. 60-66. Cooper and McCord omitted this law from their compilation.

49 See "An Act for the Governing of Negroes," (Act no. 329), in *Acts of Assembly, Passed in the Island of Barbados, From 1648, to 1718* (London: John Baskett, 1721), pp. 137-144.

50 Governor Archdale's Laws [1696], pp. 28-30. Cooper and McCord omitted this law from their compilation as well.

increased. By 1695 there were about two thousand African slaves in South Carolina, making the percentage of blacks in the province higher than in any other American mainland colony.[51]

By the end of the seventeenth century South Carolinians had surrounded their slaves with a comprehensive system of slave codes which Winthrop Jordan has called "the most rigorous deprivation of freedom to exist in institutionalized form anywhere in the English continental colonies."[52]

The South Carolina slave laws, of course, do not reflect actual practice. They set formal standards which were not always rigidly enforced. But the statutes do reflect the felt necessities of the chief slaveowners who sat in the colonial assembly and composed the laws. Their expectations, fears, and anxieties are closely woven together in the statutes. The laws take on added meaning when carefully placed within the context of early South Carolina history: the socio-economic and cultural ties to the West Indies; the continuing vitality of the Caribbean connection, facilitated by flows of goods, people, news, and ideas; the growing ratio of blacks to whites, especially in some isolated areas; and the intense political factionalism in the colony. Taken together, the South Carolina slave laws represent an historical fingerprint impressed upon the colonial landscape by the white ruling class. Placed in a local context, their underlying dimensions can reveal many subtle complexities of the emerging slave society.

51 See the anonymous and undated manuscript, "Some weighty considerations relating to America...," item 64 in Governor Archdale's Papers, mfm., South Carolina Department of Archives and History, Columbia, S.C. It states: "South Carolina hath nott above 2000 whites & those not ye wealthyest of men in Americah; yett they have procured as many or more Negroes whose labours are Equal! to ye English."

52 Jordan, *White over Black*, p. 85.

Barbadian Settlers in Early Carolina: Historiographical Notes

Kinloch Bull

Former Foreign Service officers and independent scholar living in Arlington, Virginia; he is the author of *Oligarchs in Colonial and Revolutionary Charleston: Lieutenant Governor William Bull II and His Family* (Columbia: University of South Carolina Press, 1991).

Originally published in Volume 96, Number 4 (October 1995)

The Barbadian influence always has been considered an important part of South Carolina's historical heritage, particularly in the early years after the founding of Charleston in 1670. Almost a decade before that time, some principal men in Barbados already were concerning themselves with establishing a colony in Carolina. On August 14, 1663, eighty-five gentlemen of Barbados signed a document expressing interest in the settlement of Carolina; eight Lords Proprietors obtained charters for Carolina in 1663 and 1665. A group of Barbadians under the leadership of Sir John Yeamans attempted a settlement at Cape Fear (now in North Carolina) in 1665, but the settlement did not prosper. A few of these Cape Fear settlers, including Sir John Yeamans, were among the early settlers in and around Charlestown.[1]

The number of Barbadians who sailed for Carolina in the 1670s is not known, but by the end of 1672 a majority of the settlers in Charlestown are believed to have been Barbadian. They exercised an important influence. After the beginning of the third Dutch War in 1672, with the disturbing effect of the war in the Caribbean and elsewhere, migration from Barbados to Carolina fell off sharply and appears not to have recovered until 1678. Then it dwindled almost to the vanishing point by the end of the seventeenth century.[2]

The historiography concerning the early history of Carolina and West Indian influences is considerable. Beginning in the late-nineteenth century, historians have attempted to identify the place of origin of some of the better

1 Peter F. Campbell, former president of the Barbados Museum and Historical Society and historian of seventeenth-century Barbados, states that he has found evidence of only twelve of the eighty-five Barbadian signers having gone to Carolina, and of these, four or five very likely went only for a short time. Campbell, "Early Barbadian Emigration to South Carolina," ms, Sept. 16, 1993, sent to the Campbell to the author. This and other letters from Campbell to the author are in the Barbados Miscellaneous Papers (30-8-172) in the collections of the South Carolina Historical Society (hereafter SCHS), Charleston.

2 Alfred D. Chandler, "The Expansion of Barbados," *The Journal of the Barbados Museum and Historical Society* XIII, pp. 125-136, is one of the best accounts available of the successive waves of emigration from Barbados in the late-seventeenth century, and the role played by the Barbadians in early Carolina. Chandler's article has since been republished, without the footnotes, in Peter F. Campbell, ed., *Chapters in Barbados History* (St. Ann's Garrison, Barbados: The Barbados Museum and Historical Society, 1986), pp. 61-89. Close ties between South Carolina and Barbados continued well past the end of the seventeenth century.

known settlers.[3] Barbados drew attention because it was important as a colony, and Barbadians were believed to have been the most suitable settlers because of their experience planting and living in a warm climate. "I am glad to hear soe many considerable men come from Barbados for we find by deare experience that noe other are able to make a Plantation but such as are in condition to stock and furnish themselves," wrote Lord Ashley Cooper of the Lords Proprietors to Sir John Yeamans in South Carolina.[4]

However, in 1993, Peter F. Campbell, utilizing evidence in Barbadian archives, which are more complete for the late-seventeenth century than those for South Carolina, called into question the Barbadian credentials of some early governors of Carolina. He wrote: "If one mentions South Carolina in Barbados, one is likely to hear that seven of the early Governors were Barbadians or the sons of Barbadian fathers. There were, in fact, only three Governors of South Carolina who were Barbadians or whose fathers were Barbadians."[5]

The problem Campbell identifies is that many historians have assumed that people noted in early records as having "arrived from Barbados" had been residents of Barbados when that was not necessarily the case. The easiest route from the British isles to Carolina followed the southerly trade winds to the southern West Indies. Barbados, as the easternmost island in the southern West Indies, would have been the first natural landfall, where passengers and cargo were discharged and taken on for the northern Caribbean islands and the North American mainland. Many who arrived in Charlestown only transited Barbados, which was their previous port of call and not their port of origin. In the following historiographical notes, we shall examine the origins of some of these mistaken assumptions which have been perpetuated as later historians have adopted the conclusions of their predecessors as references.

3 Langdon Cheves, ed., "The Shaftesbury Papers and other Records Relating to Carolina and the First Settlement on Ashley River Prior to the Year 1676," *Collections of the South Carolina Historical Society* Vol. 5 (Charleston, S.C.: The South Carolina Historical Society, 1897); Edward McCrady, *The History of South Carolina under the Proprietary Government 1670-1719* (New York: Macmillan, 1897; repr. Russell and Russell, 1969), pp. 327n-328n; John Hotten, *The Original List of Persons of Quality 1600-1700* (Baltimore, Md.: Genealogical Publishing Co., 1962 "Reprinted from Second Edition, 1880").

4 Chandler, "Expansion of Barbados," p. 129.

5 Campbell, *Some Early Barbadian History* (Kingston, Jamaica: Ian Randle Publishers Ltd., 1993), pp. 148-157.

There are several narratives concerning Carolina in its early years written by persons visiting or residing in Carolina at the time, but they are uninformative on names or numbers of Barbadian settlers. Early writings about South Carolina had little to say on these subjects, other than references to trade connections. But the fact that early published narratives, some perhaps best described as promotional literature, had little to say about Barbados and Barbadians does not mean that these subjects were unimportant: such accounts tended to be short, and there was no census in seventeenth-century Carolina, as there was in Barbados in 1679, to serve as a point of departure. Questions of geographic origin, cultural influences, demographic factors—these are points that were not addressed in early secondary works.[6]

The first general history of South Carolina, published in 1779 by Alexander Hewatt, a loyalist clergyman, is silent on these subjects, as are the histories of Dr. David Ramsay, published in the early 1800s, and William Gilmore Simms some four decades later.[7] William J. Rivers, in his history of South Carolina published in 1856, approached the question of the Barbadian presence very cautiously: After Sir John Yeamans of Barbados was appointed governor of South Carolina in 1672, "many of the settle rs [at Cape Fear) are said to have followed him hither.... The first accession to the number of original settlers had come from Barbadoes and Cape Fear."[8]

Important collections of historical documents relating to the history of South Carolina were published during the antebellum period, as well as in the decades which followed, which contain the texts of historical documents, and sometimes unreferenced statements of fact by the ed itor. One of the most important is the Shaftesbury papers, papers of the Lords Proprietors, edited by Langdon Cheves. Cheves claims some individuals to be Barbadians, but he fails to distinguish natives of Barbados from transit passengers. In his footnotes we find mention of Barbadian origins for two of the early governors of Carolina, Sir John Yeamans and Governor James Moore (Sr.); he is correct in the first case but not the second, as will appear below.[9]

6 Some early accounts of Carolina are included in Alexander S. Salley, ed., *Narratives of Early Carolina, 1650-1708* (New York: Barnes & Noble, 1911).

7 Alexander Hewatt, *An Historical Account of the Rise and Progress of the Colonies of South Carolina and Georgia,* 2 vols. (London: Alexander Donaldson, 1779); David Ramsay, *History of South Carolina from its Settlement in 1670 to the year 1808,* Vol. 1 (Charleston, S.C.: David Longworth, 18098); William Gilmore Simms, *The History of South Carolina* (Charleston, S.C.: S. Babcock & Co., 1840).

8 William J. Rivers, *A Sketch of the History of South Carolina* (Spartanburg, S.C.: The Reprint Co., 1972 from an 1856 ed.), p. 120.

9 Cheves, "Shaftesbury Papers," p. 47n.

To return to the subject of general histories of South Carolina, the next after that of Rivers was Edward McCrady's *The History of South Carolina under the Proprietary Government,* published in 1897. McCrady's work, like that of Cheves, frequently has been used as a reference by later historians. A lengthy footnote in McCrady's work, identifying some high-profile settlers as of Barbadian origin, contains some significant errors which have been copied by later historians. Here are some well-known names of early settlers: "In the list of emigrants from Barbados in the year 1679 we find the names of Robert Daniel[ll], Thomas Drayton, John Ladson, and Arthur Middleton—names which have since been interwoven with the history of the state."[10] McCrady gives as his source *"Emigrants to America, 1600-1700."* John Hotten had drawn upon ship lists of passengers leaving Barbados in 1679, lists forwarded by Governor Sir Jonathan Atkins of Barbados to London in 1680, together with other important information concerning the island.[11] McCrady provides the names of some other prominent early arrivals from Barbados, all in a lengthy footnote:

> Sir John Colleton, one of the Proprietors, was from Barbadoes, and so were his two brothers,James, the Governor, and Major Charles Colleton. From that island came Sir John Yeamans, the Landgrave and Governor; Captain John Godfrey, Deputy [Governor];... Robert Daniel[1], Landgrave and Governor; Arthur and Edward Middleton, Benjamin and Robert Gibbes, Barnard Schinkingh...and Alexander Skeene. Among others from Barbadoes were those of the following names:... Drayton,...Fenwicke,...Fox,...Ladson, Moore, Strode Some of these were probably but temporarily on the islands; some had been long-established residents...
>
> This list has been compiled with the assistance of Langdon Cheves, Esq., from various sources, including Emigrants to America, 1600-1700 (Hotten).[12]

Among McCrady's errors, the most prominent were in identifying members of the Colleton family. Sir John Colleton was very influential in the founding of Carolina, but died before the colony was settled in 1670. Governor James Colleton and Charles Colleton were erroneously

10 McCrady, *Proprietary Government,* p. 182.

11 John Hotten, *The Original Lists of Persons of Quality.* One of the most important of the documents enclosed by Atkins was a census of Barbados for 1679, the only census for the colony in the seventeenth century. Persons absent from the island at the time were not included in the census.

12 Ibid., pp. 327n-328n; McCrady, *Proprietary Government,* pp. 327n-328n.

identified by McCrady as his brothers, but James was a younger son and Charles was a grandson, the illegitimate son of Sir John's oldest son, Sir Peter Colleton. They were Barbadian, however, and the Colleton family remained important in the early years of the colony.[13]

Errors in identifying settlers from Barbados by later historians appear mostly to have begun with the works of McCrady and Cheves. Historians have tended to rely on their important works as their sources. A significant qualification by McCrady—"Some of these were probably but temporarily on the islands"—has been overlooked. Perhaps there have been more identifications from primary sources than now appear, but for the most part we do not know what they were or where they were found because the references to original records, in the works cited above for example, have tended to be very general. As recently as ten years ago, two prominent historians wrote that "The sources of Charleston's growth are but poorly understood; indeed, it is the least studied of the principal colonial ports, and major opportunities await its historians."[14] This would appear to apply very much to Barbadian origins.

McCrady is not known to have had access to records in Barbados (exclusive of Hotten's compilation, which he cited), but we now can see how helpful they can be. Peter Campbell has noted how extensive Barbadian records are for the early period: "If a person was a white householder in the second half of the seventeenth century, I should be surprised not to find his name occuring in a will or deed, in the census of white householders of 1679, or in the muster rolls of the militia. There are, of course, other sources."[15] Based on his years of research in Barbados, here is what he has done with the names cited by McCrady.

There is evidence in Barbadian records, writes Campbell, of the Barbadian origins of Sir John Yeamans and John Godfrey, a small planter from northern Barbados, but none for Robert Daniell.[16] Arthur Middleton was a merchant and slave trader in Barbados, but his brother Edward apparently came out from England and only stayed briefly in Barbados.[17]

13 For further information on the Colleton family in Barbados, see Campbell to Mrs. Agnes Leland Baldwin, Apr. 28, 1993, SCHS; John Buchanan, "The Colleton Family and the Early History of South Carolina and Barbados, 1646-1775," Ph.D. dissertation, University of Edinburgh, 1989.

14 John J. McCusker and Russell R. Menard, *The Economy of British America 1607-1789* (Chapel Hill: University of North Carolina Press, 1985), p. 185.

15 Campbell, *Some Early Barbadian History,* p. 150.

16 Ibid., pp. 150-151, and Campbell, "Early Barbadian Emigration."

17 Campbell, *Some Early Barbadian History,* pp. 151-152.

Gibbes came from a large Barbadian family. Schinkingh or Schenkingh (there are several variant spellings) was a merchant in Barbados, and Alexander Skene lived in Barbados for at least ten years, having been secretary of the island and private secretary to the governor.[18] No evidence has been found for Barbadian origins of Drayton, Fox, or Moore.[19] Strode was a prominent Barbados merchant who visited Carolina at times, although his home was in Barbados. His son died in Carolina in the early 1700s.[20] Ladson probably was a small merchant, and a William Fenwicke was possibly of Barbadian planter origins.[21]

The next important historical work following that of McCrady was not a history of South Carolina but of Charleston, Mrs. St. Julien Ravenel's *Charleston: The Place and the People,* and it contains some legends and folklore of the city not found elsewhere. She makes only passing mention of emigrants to Carolina from the West Indies and elsewhere, but notes that Governor James Moore (Sr.) came from Barbados, where he married the daughter of Sir John Yeamans. Mrs. Moore has been thought to have been the posthumous daughter of Lieutenant Colonel Benjamin Berringer, whose widow married Yeamans ten weeks after her husband's death.[22]

But perhaps Mrs. Ravenel got it right after all. Peter Campbell relates the history of the Berringer family in Barbados and a dark story of perjury and murder emerges, of a man (Sir John Yeamans) who fell in love with the wife of another man (Colonel Berringer). Mrs. Berringer and Sir John Yeamans murdered her husband, probably by poison. Berringer's will leaving everything to his family in England was suppressed and a nuncupative (oral) will leaving everything to Mrs. Berringer and her children was substituted, sworn to by suspect and unreliable witnesses.[23]

But Mrs. Ravenel seems to have inherited a problem in ascribing Barbadian origins to Governor James Moore, Sr., who, she writes, met and married his wife, Margaret Berringer (or Yeamans), in Barbados. We do

18 Campbell, "Early Barbadian Emigration."

19 Campbell, *Some Early Barbadian History,* pp. 157-160; Campbell, "Early Barbadian Emigration"; Campbell to author, Oct. 4, 1993, SCHS.

20 Campbell to the author, June 11, 1995, and Charles H. Lesser, *South Carolina Begins: The Records of a Proprietary Colony, 1663-1721* (Columbia: S.C. Department of Archives and History, 1995), p. 387.

21 Campbell, "Early Barbadian Emigration," and Campbell to the author, Oct. 4, 1993, SCHS.

22 Mrs. St. Julien Ravenel, *Charleston, the Place and the People* (New York: The MacMillan Co., 1912), p. 37; H.A.M. Smith, *Rivers and Regions of Early South* Carolina(Spartanburg, S.C.: The Reprint Co., 1988), p. 91 and passim. Sir John Yeamans's will in "Registry of the Secy of the Province," ms., p. 2, South Carolina Department of Archives and History (hereafter SCDAH) shows a daughter Margaret. Vere Langford, *The History of the Island of Antigua* (London: n.p., 1899) contains genealogy of the Yeamans family or families, mostly in Antigua, but it contains many errors.

23 Campbell, *Some Early Barbadian History,* pp. 115-127.

not know many of Mrs. Ravenel's sources as she did not use footnotes, with one unimportant exception. We do not know where she obtained her information about Governor Moore's alleged Barbadian origins, but it could have been from either Cheves or McCrady.[24] Campbell tells us that the wedding probably took place in Carolina, there being no evidence of its having taken place in Barbados. Their son, Governor James Moore, Jr., is believed to have been born in South Carolina; Campbell has found no evidence that he ever lived in Barbados.[25]

An influential 1930 article by John P. Thomas, Jr. in the *South Carolina Historical and Genealogical Magazine* contains the names of a considerable number of persons to whom Barbadian origins are ascribed, mostly for the period prior to 1676. High-profile emigrants named by the author include Thomas and Robert Gibbes, Arthur Middleton, and Thomas Drayton, initially sourced to McCrady, with additional citations of other works. Many of the names given by Thomas appear to have been Barbadian, but the Barbadian credentials of others appear questionable.[26]

We find these recurring errors about Barbadians in the next general history of South Carolina, that of David Duncan Wallace in 1934: "The Barbadian element [among the early settlers of Carolina] was increased by the arrival of Robert Daniel[l], Thomas Drayton...and Arthur Middleton." The inclusion of Daniell and Drayton has been questioned by Campbell, as discussed above. Wallace's footnote cites McCrady as a reference. Wallace also observed that Barbadian arrivals on the average were men of larger means and higher social standing than immigrants from England, a subject which depends initially on identifying which immigrants were authentic Barbadians, before exploring their economic and social origins.[27]

Identification problems arise again in a major work on the southern colonies in the colonial period, Jack P. Greene's *The Quest for Power*, published in 1963. Greene mentions the Middletons, the Fenwicks, Draytons, and Moores as West Indian immigrants, the first two correctly and the second two not. Greene cites McCrady as his source.[28]

24 Cheves, "Shaftesbury Papers," p. 463, and McCrady, *Proprietary Government*, p. 327n-328n.

25 Campbell, *Some Early Barbadian History*, p. 126.

26 John P. Thomas, Jr., "The Barbadians in South Carolina," *South Carolina Historicnl and Genealogical Magazine* (hereafter *SCHM)* 31 (April, 1930), pp. 75-92. Campbell has noted that of the sixty-two white Barbadian immigrants named by Thomas (p. 92), he has been able to find no trace of twenty-six of them ever having been in Barbados, and of the remainder, only a handful came from established Barbadian families. Campbell to the author, July 28, 1991.

27 David Duncan Wallace, *The History of South Carolina* (New York: American Historical Society, 1934) Vol. 1, p. 92.

28 Jack P. Greene, *The Quest for Power* (Chapel Hill: University of North Carolina Press, 1963), p. 32.

The next general history of South Carolina was *Colonial South Carolina,* by M. Eugene Sirmans, published in 1966. Sirmans underscored the importance of the Barbadian connection in his second chapter, "The Rise of the Barbadians, 1670-1682," and discussed their significance in the first decade of the colony. Some mis-identifications are present, and Cheves, McCrady, and Thomas all appear to have been contributors. The erroneous identification of two important early settlers—James Moore, Sr. and Maurice Matthews—appears to have colored Sirmans's view that an important political faction in early Carolina, the so-called Goose Creek men, was predominantly of Barbadian origin. Moore and Matthews, though leaders of this faction, were not Barbadian. Not all of the faction members lived at Goose Creek, and not all of them were Barbadian, as Sirmans made clear, but this subject could benefit from a reappraisal based on primary sources.[29]

An influential work which followed that of Sirmans was *First Settlers 1670-1700,* by Agnes Leland Baldwin. It is a listing of 3,300 people who can be documented as having been associated with, although not necessarily settled in, Carolina between 1670 and 1700. An earlier version deals only with the first decade.[30] *First Settlers* draws exclusively on primary sources, published or otherwise. In Mrs. Baldwin's work we find the origins of settlers in, or persons associated with, early Carolina to the extent they are known, but mostly they are not. Some of these people are shown as" arrived from Barbados" or from some other location, but mostly their origins are not identified.

Richard S. Dunn's *Sugar and Slaves* was published in 1972, a study of English settlers in Barbados and the other West Indian islands in the seventeenth and early-eighteenth centuries. It contains a close look at the Barbadians who settled in Carolina, particularly the governors: "Seven of the early South Carolina governors had Barbados backgrounds," he writes. Governors whom he claims had come from Barbados or whose

29 M. Eugene Sirmans, *Colonial South Carolina* (Chapel Hill: University of North Carolina Press, 1966). For Sirmans's identification of particular people as Barbadian, see pp. 27, 29, 41, and 43. For his discussion of the Goose Creek men and their political influence, see pp. 41-43 and 45-49. With regard to the Goose Creek men, Sirmans may have been influenced by Wallace, who thought the Goose Creek men were composed largely of Anglican Barbadians. Wallace, *History of South Carolina,* Vol. 1, p. 124.

30 Agnes Leland Baldwin, *First Settlers of South Carolina 1670-1700* (Easley, S.C.: Southern Historical Press, 1985). All further references to *First Settlers* by short title concern this volume and not the earlier volume which covers only the period 1670- 1680 (Baldwin, *First Settlers of South Carolina 1670-1680* [Easley, S.C.: Southern Historical Press, 1969]). Mrs. Baldwin provides sources for the names she included, and her work has valuable appendices.

father had done so were Sir John Yeamans, James Colleton, James Moore [Sr.], Robert Gibbes, Robert Daniel[l], James Moore, Jr., and Arthur Middleton. Dunn relied on Mrs. Baldwin's work, but misinterpreted what she wrote. James Moore, Jr. seems to have been included in the belief that his father, James Moore, Sr., was Barbadian, which he was not. Arthur Middleton did come from Barbados but he was not a governor. This is a genealogical error; it was Middleton's nephew Arthur Middleton who was an acting governor, 1725-1730. Only three of Dunn's seven governors can be shown to have had Barbadian backgrounds.[31]

Dunn used his interpretation of Mrs. Baldwin's work to arrive at exact numbers of Barbadians believed to have arrived in Carolina during the decade 1670-1680: "During the decade of the 1670s, 175 Barbadians can be identified as corning to the new colony. They brought with them at least 150 servants and slaves."[32] These are not valid numbers. No one knows the total number of Barbadians who arrived in Carolina in its first decade; there is no basis for more than a rough estimate.[33] There is, however, a list of all persons who departed Barbados in 1679, the only year for which we have a fairly exact number. The list was included as an attachment to Barbados Governor Atkins's famous report of 1680, and the total was 593, of whom only about thirty-eight departed for Carolina, and fewer than half of these have been identified so far as Barbadian.[34]

Colonial South Carolina by Robert M. Weir, published in 1983, does not comment very much on Barbadian settlers, but follows the lead of Dunn in statistics: "For about a third of those who arrived [in Carolina] during the first decade, the place of origin is known and about half of these came from Barbados."[35] In giving these fractions, Weir is stating them as proportions of total numbers of settlers derived by Dunn from Mrs. Baldwin's work.

31 Richard S. Dunn, *Sugar and Slaves* (Chapel Hill: University of North Carolina Press,1972), p.112 and 112n. Dunn also repeats Sirmans's undocumented suggestion that the "Goose Creek men" were predominantly Barbadian; Dunn cites Sirmans and John P. Thomas as references. See also Campbell, *Some Early Barbadian History*, pp. 148-157.

32 Dunn, *Sugar and Slaves*, p.112. Dunn cites Alfred D. Chandler, "The Expansion of Barbados," as his reference, but these numbers do not appear in Chandler and it is clear from Dunn's text that his numbers were from Mrs. Baldwin' s work.

33 Only rough estimates are available for the total population of Carolina at the end of the first decade, from accounts published by observers in the early 1680s. *Carolina; or a Description of the Present State of that Country* by T.A. [thought to be Thomas Amy or Thomas Ash] (London: Printed for W.C., 1682), p. 38, gives an estimate of 1000-1200. Sirmans offers no estimate of numbers of Barbadian settlers but writes, "By 1683 there were about 1,000 men in the colony, with some 200 families living in Charles Town." *Colonial History*, p. 24.

34 Dunn, *Sugar and Slaves*, pp. 110-112; Campbell, *Early Barbadian History*, pp. 154-156.

35 Robert M. Weir, *Colonial South Carolina* (Millwood, N.Y.: KTO Press, 1983), p. 60.

There is also a repetition of an error, or possible error, by Weir in the origins of the Goose Creek men, which can be traced back to Sirmans and to the earlier work by Wallace: "Composed by and large of Barbadian Anglicans, this faction was led by Maurice Matthews." There is an implication that Matthews was Barbadian, which he was not.[36]

A more recent work on the subject of Barbadian settlers is Richard Waterhouse's *A New World Gentry,* published in 1989. Waterhouse's numbers are not valid: here again are counts of people sourced to his interpretation of Mrs. Baldwin's work: "Of approximately 683 colonists arriving in South Carolina during the first decade of settlement, 177, amounting to almost half those whose place of origin can be identified, came from Barbados."[37]

Finally, we consider Jack P. Greene's "Colonial South Carolina and the Caribbean Connection," which appeared in the *South Carolina Historical Magazine* in 1987. He states:

> Almost half of the whites who came to the new settlement [Carolina] during the first two years were from Barbados, and this distribution continued for at least two decades. The most thorough and authoritative study we have of the 1,343 white settlers who immigrated to South Carolina between 1670 and 1690 indicates that more than 54 percent were probably from Barbados.[38]

Greene does not give his source for his numbers, or how he and his unidentified authoritative source arrived at the figure of 54 percent (725) for the Barbadians. These figures are not credible.

Historians until recently for the most part have ignored the black settlers who came to the colony in the early years as slaves, mostly from Barbados. Their names are not known and neither are their numbers,

36 Ibid., p. 65.

37 Richard Waterhouse, *A New World Gentry: The Making of a Merchant and Planter Class in South Carolina,* 1670-1770 (New York: Garland Publishing Co., 1989), p. 10. Waterhouse repeats the belief that the Goose Creek men were mostly Barbadians, citing Sirmans.

38 Jack P. Greene, "Colonial South Carolina and the Caribbean Connection," *SCHM* 88 (July 1987), pp. 192-210.

although the latter seem to have been quite small until rice from Angola, and slaves skilled in its cultivation, came to Carolina in the early 1690s.[39]

In the end, we can see that some early settlers in Carolina have been erroneously identified as Barbadians, and the reasons why this happened. The use of "arrived from Barbados" to establish Barbados as a prior place of residence may have lulled historians into a false sense of certainty, and kept some from searching for firmer evidence. Research in recent years in Barbadian archives by Peter Campbell has supported the island origin of some and discarded that of others, and still others can be identified only tentatively. In the process, a better picture has emerged of what can or cannot be substantiated from records in Barbados, what sorts of people the Barbadian emigrants were. Scholars in the United States now have more to work with with the recent publication of Barbadian will, marriage, and baptism records for the seventeenth century, and varying periods thereafter.[40] Similarly, the exact numbers stated by Richard Dunn and later historians must be discarded, as they are based on erroneous assumptions. In their place, the best rough estimates suggest that 200 or 300 Barbadians migrated to Carolina between about 1670 and 1682. In any event, the numbers do not seem as important as the kinds of people the Barbadians were. The belief that the Barbadian emigrants to Carolina included men of substance, who were somewhat higher in the social and economic scale than emigrants from Europe in the early years, has some basis in the papers of the Lords Proprietors. This was noted by Rivers in the mid-nineteenth century, elaborated upon by Dunn twenty years ago, and further commented upon most recently by Peter Campbell.

This article deals with names and numbers, and not with the broader subject of Carolina's Barbadian heritage. The importance of this heritage—whatever the numbers—is not in dispute. Further research into the evidence of Barbadian origins may well produce a richer, though perhaps more diffuse, view of this heritage.

39 Kinloch Bull, Jr., *Oligarchs in Colonial and Revolutionary Charleston: Lieutenant Governor William Bull II and His Family* (Columbia: University of South Carolina Press, 1991), p. 339; Peter H. Wood, *Black Majority: Negroes in Colonial South Carolina from 1670 through the Stono Rebellion* (New York: Alfred A. Knopf, 1974), pp. 29-31.

40 Joanne McCree Sanders, *Barbados Records,* 6 vols. (Baltimore, Md.: The Genealogical Publishing Co.,1979-1984). Land records are available only in Barbados, but they are indexed.

ERRATA

The Middletons of Barbados have caused historians difficulties for many years.

In Agnes Baldwin's first edition of *First Settlers in Barbados* she claimed that Arthur and Edward Middleton (later of South Carolina) were brothers of Thomas and Benjamin Middleton. In her second edition, she correctly disclaimed that. Nonetheless, some of the authors in this collection repeat the fictional connection.

About the Authors

Kinloch Bull ("Barbadian Settlers in Early Carolina: Historiographical Notes") was an independent scholar and longtime friend of the South Carolina Historical Society. He wrote *Oligarchs in Colonial and Revolutionary Charles- ton: Lieutenant Governor William Bull II and His Family.*

Richards Dunn ("The English Sugar Islands and the Founding of South Carolina") is the author of many titles, including *Sugar and Slaves: The Rise of the Planter Class in the English West Indies, 1625-1713.* He edited the papers of William Penn and the journal of John Winthrop.

Jack P. Greene ("Colonial South Carolina and the Caribbean Connection") has written a number of books on colonial history, including *Pursuits of Happiness: The Social Development of Early Modern British Colonies and the Formation of American Culture* and *The Quest for Power: The Lower Houses ofAssembly in the Southern Royal Colonies, 1689-1776.*

Stephen G. Hoffius ("Introduction") is a former editor of the *South Carolina Historical Magazine,* the managing editor of Home House Press, and the coauthor, with Susan Millar Williams, of *Upheaval in Charleston: Earthquake and Murder on the Eve of Jim Crow.*

Thomas J. Little ("The South Carolina Slave Laws Reconsidered, 1670- 1700") was working on his dissertation, "The Influence of the West Indies upon Slavery in Colonial South Carolina, 1670-1738," when he published this article. He received his doctorate in history from Rice University in 1989. He is now chair of the History Department at Emory and Henry University in Virginia.

George C. Rogers, Jr. ("Review of The Barbados-Carolina Connection") was one of South Carolina's most loved historians. A former editor of the South Carolina Historical Magazine, he wrote *The History of Georgetown County, South Carolina, Charleston in the Age of the Pinckneys,* and many other books about South Carolina history.

John P. Thomas, Jr. was a professor at the University of South Carolina Law School. Transcriptions of many of his lectures to social clubs are among the collections of the South Caroliniana Library at the University of South Carolina. The Historical Commission of South Carolina published his biography of botanist Thomas Walter in 1946.

George W. Williams ("Review of The Barbados-Carolina Connection") taught English at Duke University, but always came back to Charleston. He wrote *St. Michael's, Charleston, 1751-1951,* and then fifty years later prepared the revised edition.

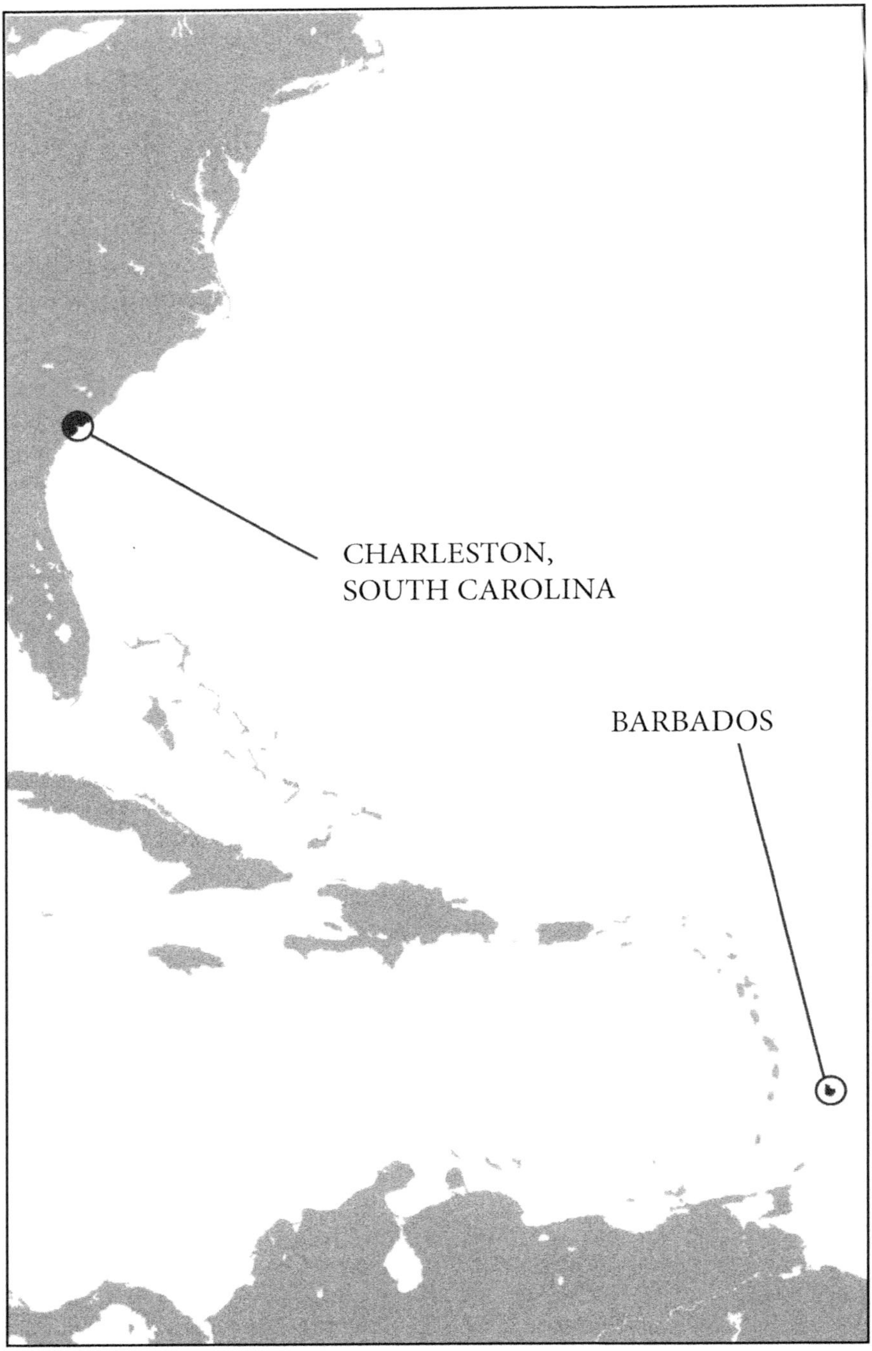
CHARLESTON,
SOUTH CAROLINA
BARBADOS

Index

A

"Act for the Better Ordering of Slaves," 70- 73
"Act Inhibiting Trading between Servants and Slaves," 65-68, 71, 72
Adventure, 5
Albemarle, 11
Albemarle Point, settlement of, 12
alcohol, in Jamaica, 28-29
Alleyne, Warren, and Henry Fraser, *The Barbados-Carolina Connection*, 53-57
Antigua, 20, 23, 40, 44 Archdale, John, 9n13, 73
Archdale, Thomas, 9n13
architecture, in Barbados, 29-30, 54-57. *See also* single house.
Arlington House (Speightstown, Bar.), viii, 56-57
Ashley River, 12, 15
Atkins, Jonathan, 78, 83
Axtell, _____, 15

B

Bahamas, 20
Baldwin, Agnes Leland, 19, 21-22, 82-84
Baptists, 64, 69
Barbados; early history of, 1-3, 34-37; emigration from, 21-22, 75-85; fire (17, 66); health in, 24-26,41,43; Jews in, 25n12; parish names, 16, 17; poor whites in, 22; slaves in, 16, 41, 43; 1679 census, 78n11, 79; population of, 20, 21, 36, 41, 43; South Carolina legislature contributed relief funds to, 17; wealth in, 36, 43
The Barbados-Carolina Connection, by Warren Alleyne and Henry Fraser, 53-57
Barbados Ministry of Tourism Authority, vii
Barbados Museum and Historical Society, vii
Barbados Police Band, viii
Barbados-Carolina Committee (Barbados Ministry of Tourism Authority), vii
Bay Mansion (Barbados), 55
Bedon, George, 18n20
Beresford family, 15
Berkeley, John, 4
Berkeley, William, 4
Bermuda, 11, 20
Berringer family, 22n7
Berringer, Benjamin, 14
Berringer, Margaret, 13-14, 81
Berrow, Christopher, 18n20
Black Carolina Corps, viii
Black Majority, by Peter Wood, vii
Blake, Joseph, 9n13, 15
Bonnet, Stede, 54
Boswood, Sam, 18n20
Bowen, Richmond, 53-54
Brewton, Miles, 18n20
Bridenbaugh, Carl, 54
Bridenbaugh, Roberta, 54
Bridgetown (Barbados), 29-30, 56
Brighton House (Barbados), 55
Broughton, Thomas, 19n3
Bull's Bay, 11
Burnet, Joan, 18n20
Bush Hill House (Barbados), viii
Butler, Charles, 15

C

Campbell, Peter, 76, 79-81, 85; "Early Barbadian Emigration to South Carolina," 75n1
Cantey family, 18n20
Cardross, Lord, 15
Carolina, 11-12, 18n20
Carolina; 16th-century settlement of, 3n4; 17th-century settlement of, 3-18, 21-24, 38
Carolina-Caribbean Association, vii, viii
Carolina Lowcountry and the Atlantic World program, vii
Carr, William, 18n20
Carteret, George, 4, 18n20
Cartwright, George. *See* Carteret, George
Cassique of Kiawah, 7-8, 11-12
Chandler, Alfred D., 83n32
Charles, 18n20
Charleston, S.C., founding of, 12; Oyster Point laid out, 13
chattel houses, 55
Cheves, Langdon, ed. *The Shaftesbury Papers*, vii, 5, 13, 77-79, 81, 82
Church of England, 2, 14, 15
Chume, A., 18n20
clothing, in Jamaica, 29
Clutterbuck family, 22n7
Codrington College, Principal's Lodge (Barbados), 55
Cole, John, 18n20
Colleton family, 18n20, 22n7, 23- 24, 24n8
Colleton, Charles, 14, 78-79
Colleton, James, 14, 19n3, 23-24, 39,66-67,69, 78-79
Colleton, John, 4, 5, 9n13, 21, 23, 67n23, 78-79
Colleton, Peter, 5, 6, 23, 66n23, 79
Colleton, Thomas, 23, 66n23
Collins, J., 18n20
Comerten, Philip, 18n20
Cooper River, 15
Cooper, Anthony Ashley, earl of Shaftesbury, 4, 8, 12, 13, 20, 76
Copen, Samuel, "Prospect of Bridgetown in Barbados," 29- 30, 56
Corporation of the Barbadian Adventurers, 5-6
Craven, Charles, 9n13
Craven, William, 4
Cuba, 51
Culpeper, John, 13, 18n20

D

Dalton, Joseph, 11
Daniell, Robert, 9n13, 14, 19n3, 78, 79, 81, 83
Davies family, 22n7
Dearsley, Robert, 15
de Avelés, Pedro Menendez, 3n4
de Quexos, Pedro, 3n4, 6n6
de Rojas, Hernando Manrique, 3n4
dialects, 54
diets, in Jamaica, 28-29
Donne, Robert, 11
Donohoe, James, 18n20
Dowden family, 22n7
Dowden, Joseph, 18n20
Drax Hall (Barbados), 53
Drayton family, 15, 18n20, 78, 80, 81-82
Drayton, John, 51
Drayton, Thomas, 54, 78, 81
Dunn, Richard S., 19-32, 82-83, 85

E

"Early Barbadian Emigration to South Carolina," by Peter Campbell, 75nl
Edisto River, 15
Elliott family, 15, 22n7
Emigrants to America, 1600-1700, by John Hotten, 78-79

F

Fabian, Peter, 6n6
Faulconer, John, 18n20
Fenwick family, 22n7, 81. *See also* Fenwicke family
Fenwicke family, 15, 78. *See also* Fenwick family
Fenwicke, William, 80
Finden, Thomas, 18n20
Fitzpatrick, B., 18n20
Flower, Moses, 18n20
Foster family, 15, 22n7
Foster, John, 18n20
Fox family, 15, 78, 80
Fraser, Henry, and Warren Alleyne, *The Barbados-Carolina Connection*, 53-57
French Huguenots, 15, 64
"Fundamental Constitutions" of Carolina, 8; slave laws in, 60, 64, 66, 68-69, 72

G

Gibbes family, 22n7
Gibbes, Benjamin, 15, 78, 80
Gibbes, Robert, 9n13, 15, 18n20, 19n3, 39, 78, 80, 81, 83
Gibbes, Thomas, 18n20, 39, 81
Gibbon family, 15
Gilbert, James, 18n20
Godfrey,John, 14, 18n20, 78, 79
Gordillo, Francisco, 3n4, 6n6
Gray, Thomas, 14
Green, Rhoda, viii
Greene, Jack P., 33-52, 81, 84
Griffin, John, 18n20
Guadeloupe, 51

H

Hall family, 22n7
Hall, Gyles, 14, 18n20
Hare family, 15
Hayden family, 15
health; in Barbados, 24-26, 41, 43; in South Carolina, 49
Heath, Robert, 3-4
Hewatt, Alexander, 77
Hicks, Evenezer, 27
Hilton Head Island, S.C., 6
Hilton, William, 5-6, 53
Holton, Thomas, 18n20
Hotten, John, *Emigrants to America, 1600-1700*, 78-79
Howell, Enoch, 18n20
Hughes, H, 18n20
Hyde, Edward, earl of Carendon, 4

J

Jackson, Original, 18n20
Jamaica, 20-21, 25, 63n13; alcohol in, 28-29; clothing in, 29; diets in, 28-29; population in, 45-46; slaves in, 27-30, 63; sugar industry in, 44-45; supported American grievances, 50; wealth in, 27-30, 37-38, 44-45
John and Thomas, 18n20
Johnson, Nathaniel, 9n13, 19n3, 21
Johnson,Robert, 9n13, 19n3
Jones, John, 18n20
Jones, Philip, 18n20
Jordan, Winthrop, 74

K

Kyrle, Richard, 9n13

L

Ladson family, 15, 78
Ladson,John,39, 78, 80
Lake family, 15, 22n7
Lane family, 22n7
Laurens, Henry, 42
Leeward islands, 36-37, 43; population, 45-46
Ligon, Richard, 22, 54-57
Locke, John, 8, 18n20
Long, Anthony, 6n6
Long, Samuel, 27
Lords Proprietors, 4, 5, 6, 9n12, 13
Lowndes, Rawlins, 40
Lucas, Samuel, 18n20
Ludwell, Philip, 9n13, 71-72

M

Marshall, James, 18n20
Marshall, Ralph, 11
Martinique, 51
Matthews, Maurice, 18n20, 82, 83
Maverick, John, 14, 18n20
McCrady, Edward, 78-79, 81, 82
Merrick family, 22n7
Middleton family, 22n7, 23, 81
Middleton, Arthur (nephew), 83
Middleton, Arthur (uncle), 14, 18n20, 19n3, 22, 23, 39, 78, 79, 81, 83
Middleton, Benjamin (father), 22
Middleton, Benjamin (son), 23
Middleton, Edward, 14, 22, 23, 39, 78, 79
Modyford, Thomas, 5, 6, 37, 38
Monck, George, duke of Albemarle, 4
Montserrat, 20, 44
Moore family, 15, 78, 80, 81-82
Moore, James, Jr., 19n3, 81, 83
Moore, James (Sr.), 9n13-10n13, 18n20, 19n3, 78, 80, 81, 82
Morgan, Henry, 30
Morton, Joseph, 9n13, 15, 65-66
Murrell, William, 18n20

N

Native Americans; see Cassique of Kiawah
Needham, James, 18n20
Nevis, 20, 44
Nicholls Building (Bridgetown, Barbados), 57
Norris, Thomas, 18n20
Norton, John, 18n20

P

Pattison, Thomas, 18n20
Pendarvis, Joseph, 18n20
Pinckney, Eliza Lucas, 40, 46
Pinckney, Thomas, 21
Pinke, John, 18n20
pirates, 54
Poore, Richard, 18n20
Population; Barbados, 20, 21, 36, 41, 43, 78n11, 79; Jamaica, 45-46; Leeward Islands, 44; South Carolina, 38, 40, 47, 51, 62, 64
Port Royal, 11
Portman, Christopher, 14, 18n20
Presbyterians, 15, 64
Pringle, Robert, 42
"Prospect of Bridgetown in Barbados," by Samuel Copen, 29-30, 56
provision grounds, 63-64
Puerto Rico, 51

Q

Quakers, 64, 69
Quary, Robert, 9n13
Quelch, Benjamin, 39
Quintyne family, 22n7

R

Ramsay, David, 77
Ratcliff, John, 18n20
Ravenel, St. Julien, Mrs., 80-81
Ribaut, Jean, 3n4
rice, in South Carolina, 46
Rivers, William J., 77, 85
Robert, Edward, 18n20
Robinson family, 22n7
Robinson, John, 18n20
Rouffi, Guillaume, 3n4
Rowser, Richard, 18n20

S

St. Domingue, 51
St. Kitts, 20, 40, 44
St. Lucy Parish, Barbados, 54
St. Nicholas Abbey (Barbados), viii, 53
Salley, A.S., 12
Sandford family, 22n7
Sandford, Robert, 7-8, 10
Santee River, 15
Sayle, William, 9n13, 10-12, 19n3
Schenckingh/Schinkingh, Barnard/ Bernard, 15, 18n20, 39, 78, 80
Scottish dissenters, 15
Seaview Hotel (Hastings, Barbados), 56
The Shaftesbury Papers, edited by Langdon Cheves, vii, 5, 13, 77-79, 81, 82
Simms, William Gilmore, 54, 77
single house, 54-56
Sirmans, M. Eugene, 19, 82
Skene/Skeene, Alexander, 15, 78, 80
slave codes, in Barbados, 16, 59-74; in South Carolina, 16, 48, 59-74
slave executions; in Barbados, 68, 69n29, 72; in Jamaica, 69n29; in Leeward islands, 69n29
slave rebellions; in Jamaica, 68; in Barbados, 72
slavery, 15-16; in Barbados, 59-74; in Jamaica, 27-30, 44, 63; in South Carolina, 47-48, 59-74
slaves, South Carolina; laws concerning, 59-74
Sloane, Hans, 30
Smith, Paul, 11
Smith, Thomas, Jr., 14
Smith, Thomas, 9n13, 72-73
Sothel, Seth, 9n13, 69, 71
South Carolina; exports to West Indies, 41-42; health in, 49; imports from West Indies, 41- 42; military titles in, 16-17; parish names, 16; population of, 38, 40, 47, 51, 62, 64; slaves in, 47-48; trade with West Indies, 41-42; wealth in, 48-49
South Carolina National Heritage Corridor, vii
Spencer, Oliver, 18n20
Strode family, 15, 78, 80
Strode, Hugh, 18n20, 80
sugar planters, in Barbados and Jamaica, 19-31
Symonds, H., 18n20 Thomas, John P., Jr., 81, 82

T

Thompson family, 15
Thompson, George, 18n20
Thomson, Thomas, 18n20
Tookerman, Catherine, 18n20
Tookerman, Richard, 18n20
Tynte, Edward, 9n13

U

UNESCO, World Heritage List, viii
University of the West Indies, vii

W

Wallace, David Duncan, 81
Walley, William, 14
Walter family, 15
Washington, George, viii, 2
Waterhouse, Richard, 84
wealth in South Carolina, 48-49
Weir, Robert M., 83-84
West, Joseph, 10, 9n13, 12-14
West, Samuel, 11
Williams, Harriet, 53
Witty, Thomas, 18n20
Wood, Henry, 18n20
Wood, Peter, *Black Majority*, vii
Woodward family, 15
Woodward, Henry, 12, 18n20, 53

Y

Yeamans family, 22n7
Yeamans, John (father), 5
Yeamans, John (son), viii, 5, 9n13, 18n20, 19n3,53, 62, 76, 78-80, 83; death of, 14; organized expedition to Carolina 6-7 10-11; settled in Carolina, 12-13;
Yeamans, Margaret, 13-14, 80n22, 81

Printed in Great Britain
by Amazon

26313475R00061